FEEDING THE MIDDLE CLASSES

Taste, Class and Domestic Food Practices

Kate Gibson

BRISTOL
UNIVERSITY
PRESS

First published in Great Britain in 2024 by

Bristol University Press
University of Bristol
1-9 Old Park Hill
Bristol
BS2 8BB
UK
t: +44 (0)117 374 6645
e: bup-info@bristol.ac.uk

Details of international sales and distribution partners are available at bristoluniversitypress.co.uk

© Bristol University Press 2024

British Library Cataloguing in Publication Data
A catalogue record for this book is available from the British Library

ISBN 978-1-5292-1488-8 hardcover
ISBN 978-1-5292-1489-5 ePub
ISBN 978-1-5292-1490-1 ePdf

Cover design: Hayes Design and Advertising
Front cover image: 123rf/followtheflow
Bristol University Press use environmentally responsible print partners.
Printed and bound in Great Britain by CPI Group (UK) Ltd, Croydon, CR0 4YY

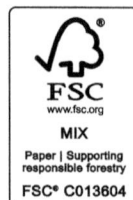

FSC
www.fsc.org
MIX
Paper | Supporting
responsible forestry
FSC® C013604

Contents

List of Figures and Table

Figures

Table

Acknowledgements

I am thankful to a number of people for the ideas that I put forward in this book. First of all, I am indebted to my participants who generously invited me into their homes and shared their stories with me. Without their contributions, this book would not have been possible.

I am indebted to several colleagues, in particular Cate Degnen, Lisa Garforth, and Alison Stenning who provided critical insight, encouragement, and advice while I undertook this research, which started life as a PhD funded by the Economic and Social Research Council. I also want to thank Suzanne Moffatt, Tessa Pollard and Katie Brittain, who have supported me in many ways as an early career researcher.

I am grateful to the anonymous reviewers for their feedback and the team at Bristol University Press who were enthusiastic about the book from the outset.

And finally, I owe an enormous thank you to my family and friends. They have listened, provided childcare and always believed in my ability to undertake this journey. In particular, my children, Billy and Ella, have been so patient and supportive. They have been, and continue to be, my inspiration.

1

Introduction

Fiona: So yeah, parsley, smoked black pudding. I bought that. I don't even like it. But [husband] does, but he hasn't eaten it yet. So, I don't know … hummus, cheese, grilled artichokes, um there's other cheeses, double Gloucestershire and then there's a funny one that I hadn't heard of before, so I bought to see what it was like. It's called Montagnulo. Eggs, butter, peach juice, sweet chilli stir-fry? [Husband] must have bought that. Butter, more cheese, yoghurt … champagne (laughs).

Jane: A bottle of wine, hazelnut milk, cause I try and avoid where I can cow's milk cause it just doesn't feel right. *Just the usuals* … lots of sauces and things to make things with. So satay sauce, mango pickle, em, the tahini for my hummus, just … I don't know what to tell you really about it. It's not that riveting. I can't stand the em gherkins … Branston, lots of em chutney cause I do like my cheese. Em let's see, natural yoghurt. I have natural yoghurt on my breakfast sometimes. What else is there? Tonic to go with the gin, lots of cheese, some fresh herbs, some cheese, 'cause I could just eat cheese really. I'm happy just to eat cheese. Em, my sourdough starter cause I like to bake. So that comes out every now and then, gets fed and goes back in again. [Italics added for emphasis]

Food is a biological necessity; we need to eat to live. But living through food extends beyond sustaining our bodies with the nutrients it provides. The materiality of food also sustains a range of social and cultural arrangements, including relations of power. What we eat, or not, carries social messages about social categories such as nationality, gender, ethnicity, and class and as such is central to our identity. While some things are naturally inedible, some things are culturally and socially disgusting.

This book is about food and class, the middle classes to be more specific. Consider these two narrative descriptions. They come from two of the 27 middle-class participants who contributed to this study. I had asked them if they could talk me through the contents of their refrigerators. At face value, they appear to be just that: lists of foods in a fridge. However, closer scrutiny of these descriptions lays bare a whole range of wider social and cultural processes and meanings. Starting with Fiona, we learn that she buys black pudding for her partner, despite her distaste for it, and that she is open to trying new foods. We learn that while her fridge contains several global foods, which she confidently lists, she questions the presence of pre-packaged sweet chilli stir-fry sauce. She concludes the narrative by jokingly pointing towards a bottle of champagne. With Jane, we learn that she differentiates between cow's milk, which 'doesn't feel right', and cheese, which she happily eats despite the obvious contradiction. We learn that she enjoys baking and spends time on it – the feeding of the sourdough starter is a continual process. What is particularly interesting is that the descriptions Fiona and Jane employ, position the foods listed as ordinary. They are 'just the usuals', as Jane suggests. Throughout this research, I was shown a range of household foods, some of which were expensive and specialist and required specific culinary knowledge and commitment. But despite these foods being anything but ordinary, their positioning as unremarkable highlights the salient ways that food practices can be normalized. I want to explore how class is implicated in this process.

The contemporary British foodscape

British consumers are selecting foods from a marketplace which is positioned as offering an abundance of diversity, such as local, exotic, artisan, plant-based, and ethical foods. We are invited as consumers to engage with and *decipher* the virtues of such foods. However, 'the capacity to see (*voir*) is a function of the knowledge (*savoir*)' (Bourdieu 1984: 2, italics original). Moreover, the consumerist framing of foods is contradictory and continually shifting. For instance, UK food trends for 2022 list 'borderless freestyle' (a trend which draws on global travel to fuse international cuisines) alongside 'climatarianism' (a diet which prioritizes reducing carbon footprints) and 'bottled cocktails' alongside 'potato milk' (Waitrose and Partners 2021). At face value, this variation in food suggests equality and inclusivity, effectively locating the field of food consumption as a democratic space (Johnston and Baumann 2014). But there are principles at work in the juxtaposition of apparently banal, exotic, eclectic and contradictory foods alongside one another, which presuppose a consumer orientation to distinguish between the culinary options presented. These principles work on the assumption that some choices are legitimate and some are illegitimate. This has the effect of validating a narrow range of foods from the apparent endless possibilities presented to consumers. This is about more than economic cost; food is as much a cultural commodity as it is an economic one. As an object of fashion, the virtues of different foods are often short-lived. As they filter down to the mainstream, they are then reclassified as common, ordinary, and unremarkable. Once in the realms of the masses, they become excluded and invalidated as a marker for distinction (Bourdieu 1984). Thus, food trends are classed although not all are named as such, and while food concerns are typically expressed in terms of health, food consumption is as much a social marker as it is a predictor of health.

From concerns about rising costs of food through to concerns about overeating, food is the subject of much academic, political, media, and public discussion. The relationship between food and poverty is well established (Green et al 2009; Parsons 2015; Garthwaite 2016; Wills and O'Connell 2018; O'Connell et al 2019). For instance, the shocking increase in foodbank use under austerity Britain has been exacerbated by the COVID-19 pandemic (Trussell Trust 2022).[1] These studies have effectively pointed out that political and public stories about class and food overwhelmingly focus on marginalized people eating the 'wrong' kinds of foods and hence reproduce an assumed binary of 'good' food and bad food, which is predominantly accessed by marginalized groups. In 2006, for example, extreme media images showed working-class mothers, known as 'sinner ladies', posting takeaway food through the fences of Rawmarsh School allegedly protesting against school meal reforms (Fox and Smith 2011). The political, public and media outcries which ensued were laced with classed and gendered disgust centred on their moralized failings.

Little has changed since, and food clearly remains a site of political struggle and judgement. Indeed, BBC journalist Michael Buerk said about overweight people: 'Give them the facts to make informed decisions; by all means "nudge" all you like, but in the end leave couch potatoes alone. They're weak, not ill' (in Moore 2019). But obesity is seen as a working-class issue, and public health research consistently documents its prevalence with socio-economic 'deprivation' (NHS Digital 2020). Placing such research in relation to rhetoric which blames obesity on moral laxity and lack of individual responsibility, its higher rates in working-class communities then becomes understood as evidence of their individual and moral 'weakness' to invest in the body through food. Equally, despite the mounting evidence that issues such as food insecurity are deeply embedded in socio-economic context, such inequalities are consistently framed as problems which are manifestations of individual or family inadequacies or failures to live within

---

[1] The Trussell Trust, who support over 1200 foodbanks in the UK, provided over two million emergency food parcels between April 2021 and March 2022, an increase of 81 per cent from 2016 to 2017 (Trussell Trust 2022).

their means (Wills and O'Connell 2018). As Jensen (2018) reminds us, political debate does not centre on the issue of poverty, but rather a 'culture of poverty' which firmly positions marginalized people as the problem. This in turn 'disguises and obscures the structural processes and excesses that are widening social inequality and deepening the poverty of those marginalised at the bottom' (Jensen 2018: 16).

What's more, not only does a consistent focus on deprivation act as a moral and discursive shorthand which fixes those living in poverty in a position of exclusion and deficit (Gidley and Rooke 2010), but it also problematically reproduces the idea that class only operates in relation to lack of access and exclusion. Public stories about 'good' food rarely consider how socio-economic and cultural inequalities *enable* access to certain foods. This is aside from the media's occasional ironic lamenting about middle-class obsessions with particular foods that often retrospectively acquire the 'healthy' label, such as porridge, quinoa, avocado and chia seeds.[2] Otherwise, consumers who engage with valued food are discursively and often unreflexively positioned as 'mindful' and 'health-conscious' (Bee 2018, *The Times;* Thompson, 2017, *MailOnline*) and implicitly valorized. Media ways of talking about food are deeply individualized. It may be tempting to think about terms such as 'health-consciousness' or 'mindful eating' as harmless or banal, yet to do so fails to recognize that access to valorized foods is often the preserve of those who are situated in privileged spaces in a classed social hierarchy. This book aims to redress this imbalance. Through its focus on those with access to resources, I seek to disentangle and examine the moral and political underpinnings of judgements made about food choice and consumption, and more specifically explore how these tensions play out in middle-class homes. In short, I explore how class is done through food.

Valued identities

> *Dis-moi ce que tu manges, je te dirai ce que tu es* (Tell me what you eat, I will tell you what you are).
>
> Brillat-Savarin, 1826

Individual responsibility is at the heart of neoliberal consumer culture. There is an assumption that what we consume is a result of individual reflexive choice and that what we 'are' is understood to be an embodiment of what we

---

[2] For example, see newspaper headlines such as 'Oat cuisine: how porridge got posh' (Salter 2016, *The Guardian*); 'To av and to hold: middle-class millennials now proposing with avocados in bizarre new trend' (Curley 2018, *The Sun*), and 'How Posh is your store cupboard? The best jars and tinned food' (Crouch 2021, *The Times*).

consume. Thus, we are positioned by what we eat; but our ability to attach value to our food practices depends on our access to resources to mark our ways of eating as legitimate. As Skeggs (2005, 2011) reminds us, neoliberal ideas of valued personhood operate around self-investment which requires economic and cultural capital. My primary concern in *Feeding the Middle Classes* is to use food to explore how class works to mark identities as valued. I explore how eating is related to identity, class positionality, and the use, and reproduction of, capital in all its forms. This is against a burgeoning backdrop of work which posits that in order it address class inequality, it is necessary to critique the assumption that middle-class taste and practice carry inherent value (Skeggs 2004a, 2004b; Lawler 2005; Reay et al 2011; Savage 2015; Reay 2017, 2018). As Tyler remarks, a perquisite for the self-investment required for the 'normative middle-class self' (2015: 500) is a rich portfolio of exchangeable cultural and economic resources. This book explores the role of food in this portfolio, as form of 'culinary capital' (Naccarato and LeBesco 2012), which through interaction with prevailing values and ideologies can confer status and power on those who recognize, possess and display it. By rethinking and unpacking the notion of middle-class reproduction through food, I problematize the normalization of middle-class practice.

In *Feeding the Middle Classes* I mobilize contemporary reframings of Bourdieusian class analysis as a lens through which to empirically focus on the material-social practices of domestic food consumption. Pierre Bourdieu's seminal work *Distinction* (1984), a landmark study conducted in 1960s France, brought to light the ways in which cultural competence and disposition are revealed through taste and consumption. That is, taste is not merely a matter of individual preference; it carries stakes, not least the maintenance of class boundaries. Within the Bourdieusian tradition, there is a burgeoning sociological interest in food (see for example, Mellor et al 2010; Naccarato and LeBesco 2012; Johnston and Baumann 2014; Cappellini et al 2015, 2016b; Paddock 2016; Kennedy et al 2019; Oncini 2020; Ehlert 2021; Yalvac and Hazir 2021). This work focuses on 'foodies' (Cairns et al 2010; Johnston and Baumann 2014, 2007), ethical eating (Johnston et al 2011; Johnston et al 2012; Kennedy, Baumann and Johnston 2019), 'alternative' foods (Paddock 2016), shopping (Cappellini et al 2016b), cosmopolitan tastes (Cappellini et al 2015), gender (Parsons 2015) and some of this work specifically focuses on home-based food practices. For instance, Mellor et al (2010) demonstrate how middle-class friendships are 'done' through dinner parties, used by individuals to exchange and display cultural capital and to bond and differentiate through shared class boundary making and the drawing of distinctions. Cairns et al (2010) find that the 'foodie' discourse offers opportunities to both contest and reinscribe gender norms. However, class boundaries are reproduced since it requires economic and cultural capital 'to make every meal "count"'

(Cairns et al 2010: 599). Studies such as these are useful because they analyse consumption at the level of a relationship of exchange and value, highlighting the link between consumption and taste and its subsequent role in maintaining social relationships.

What all these literatures have in common is that they attend to the unique way that food tastes and practices act as expressions of cultural capital, which in turn maintain classed boundaries, identities and social status. Here I explore the subtle nature of cultural distinction and social reproduction in everyday practices of sharing food in the home, and the consequences of this on the doing and making of the contemporary, middle-class family. My way into these dynamics is to employ Bourdieu's concept of habitus. Habitus captures the 'circular causality' (Bourdieu 2001: 56) between classed social structures and the individual (often unconscious) dispositions that they produce. It provides a frame of reference to explore how classed social relations are embodied in continuous dialogue with an individual's position and journey through social space. Accordingly, then, class is expressed and negotiated through everyday practice. There is a paucity of research which utilizes habitus as a theoretical lens to unpack our classed relationship to food (Beagan et al 2015). Following Beagan et al, I foreground habitus to understand how food practices and dispositions act to reproduce classed social structures because it provides a way to see the common-sense nature of food, that is, why some foods 'just *feel* right, whereas others don't' (Beagan et al 2015: 12).

Taking this Bourdieusian lead, I start from the proposition that 'good' taste is associated with middle-class lifestyles (Bourdieu 1984), and based on research with 27 middle-class participants in North East England, I argue that, while presented as innately 'classless' (Johnston et al 2011), 'good' food is code for 'middle-class' food. I follow Savage's advice that

> It is now necessary to invoke a much more subtle kind of class analysis, a kind of forensic, detective work, which involves tracing the print of class in areas where it is faintly written. Above all, the innocence, the kind of unacknowledged normality of the middle class needs to be carefully unpicked and exposed. (2003: 536–537)

In what follows, I examine the intricate connections between domestic food consumption, class and identity. I consider how class is configured in relation to individual identities by focusing on consumption at two of its most intimate points: in the home and on the body. More specifically, I focus on middle-class food practices so as to better understand the processes through which class relations are made, in particular the ways in which food works to reproduce class distinction. Placing analytical focus on valued identities allows me to 'unpick and expose' otherwise unproblematized categories by looking at the conditions in which the categories are formed in the first place. Importantly then, focusing on how the effects of class reproduce certain practices as legitimate, in turn helps disentangle how the practices of those who are excluded are devalued. In doing so, I elaborate new ways of understanding the social rules relating to 'good' taste, thus revealing how 'class operates to define and normalise certain selfhoods' (Olliver 2011: 25).

Finding out: kitchen tours and talk

The ideas underpinning this book were generated via a range of research techniques conducted over two waves of research interactions with 27 participants over 12 months of fieldwork. Methods included informal interviews, food biographies, photo voice and kitchen 'go-alongs' (Kusenbach 2003). The research was approved by Newcastle University's ethics procedures. All participants provided informed consent. Data have been anonymized, with identifiers changed and pseudonyms given to participants and other people discussed.

The participants

Participants were recruited via recruitment flyers delivered to locations identified as likely to recruit middle-class participants, such as private schools and houses in affluent areas. The research's recruitment flyer did not specifically request participation from the 'middle classes' because I did not wish to *only* recruit those who define and recognize themselves in class terms and potentially exclude rich stories relating to the complexities of class identity. Indeed, as we shall see, several participants were recruited into this research who possessed a rich portfolio of capital, yet did not identify with being middle class, often preferring to anchor themselves in a working-class history.

Participants completed a basic demographic questionnaire at first interview. Adopting a simple class framework developed from Bourdieu's use of capital, the questionnaire was used to contextualize participants' stock of economic and institutionalized cultural capital and to monitor the sample for age, area of residence, gender, household structure and ethnicity. As recruitment unfolded it became apparent that a diverse sample of participants was coming forward to participate for all of these characteristics except ethnicity and gender. While I purposefully delivered leaflets to households in ethnically-mixed areas in an attempt to improve the ethnic diversity of the sample, this yielded no results. Given the predominantly white ethnic composition of the North East (Office for National Statistics 2022), further strategies for recruiting non-white middle-class participants were not pursued. There is certainly scope to prioritize a diverse representation of race and ethnicity in future research. The inclusion of a more diverse group could help unpack the classed links between 'good taste' and ethnicity. This is especially so, since this and other research (Johnston and Baumann 2007, 2014; Atkinson and Deeming 2015; Oleschuk 2017) has established that the performance of 'good' food often entails an assumed knowing and doing of 'ethnic' foods via discourses of authenticity.

Given the well-documented relevance of gender in relation to performances around food, I instead actively prioritized addressing the gender imbalance of the sample via additional strategies to recruit male participants (initially only three male respondents had been recruited). These additional strategies I adopted for recruiting more men were also difficult and yielded modest results. Nevertheless, I persisted with securing more male participation since recruiting a mixture of male and female respondents was particularly important for analysis of potential themes relating to gender. A lack of male participation in research into food practices has been reported elsewhere (Beagan et al 2015). Indeed, the passivity of male participation extended well beyond the point of recruitment into the fieldwork as later chapters will demonstrate.

Bar one, all participants occupied objective middle-class positions. There were 11 male participants and 16 female participants. Participant ages ranged from 26 to 81 years old. All participants were white, yet not all were white British: two participants identified as Jewish and two participants were born in other countries (France and New Zealand). Aside from two of the female participants who worked part time, all participants who were in employment during the research worked full time in professional roles. The remaining participants were retired and had all previously worked in professional positions. Participant occupations included architects, teachers, accountants, graphic designers and senior managerial roles. Participants were from a range of household and family structures. These included grandparents, households with dependent or adult-aged children who were at university or had left home, blended families, lone parents, couples, and two participants lived alone. Most participants lived in areas within five miles of Newcastle upon Tyne, a locality which has undergone socio-cultural shifts in recent years resulting in what Hollands and Chatterton describe as 'a battleground between the old, industrial, and the newer, "chic", face of a more diverse, post-industrial city' (2002: 293). Interestingly, only six participants originated from the North East of England. The remaining participants moved to the area either to attend university or for employment post-university.

This sample of 27 participants certainly is not a homogenous set of people; they demonstrate as many differences as they do similarities. And so it is difficult to consistently discipline the use of the word class in this book because class is complicated. Classed groupings are of course fragmented and non-monolithic, and the participants who contributed to this research all have complex biographies. Nevertheless, my participants shared similar levels of capital, participated in similar lifestyles and voiced similar values, especially, as it turns out, in relation to food. They shared a similar middle-class position, and to not acknowledge class in this way reproduces rhetoric which places the effects of class on to individual selves. Furthermore, while I acknowledge that there are issues with referring to class as a collective, as the following chapters show, middle-classness often relies on the negative construction of a classed mass. Hence, while for many participants class played a relatively small, albeit important, part in their sense of themselves, I refer to this diverse collection of individuals as middle class. For ease of reference, Table 1.1 details participants' age ranges and pseudonyms to which, from this point on, I attach their stories.

Fieldwork: wave one

The first point of contact with participants involved an interview lasting between one and two hours. Participants described their household, current food practices (shopping, cooking, planning, preparing food, and mealtimes) and attitudes to food. In addition, inspired by Spencer and Pahl's (2006) research into 'personal communities', participants plotted people (or sets of people) with whom they shared food or provided with food in the home onto a 'map' of concentric circles. These relationships were then discussed one-by-one and prompted discussion around family meals, dinner parties and eating alone for example. Later in the interview, participants shared life histories, focusing on the role of food in their biographies. The socio-historical vantage point of participant biographies shared via the lens of food connected their identity to the social world through the process of personal history. Food is an ideal site to explore memory, particularly 'the unconscious (perhaps embodied) memories of subjects, how a sense of historicity shapes social processes and meanings, nostalgia for a real or imagined past, and invented traditions' (Holtzman 2006: 363). Life stories thus captured the extent to which our practices and perceptions remain within the limits of our primary socialization. Moreover, life history interviews allowed for the exploration of continuity and change in food dispositions at different life stages and for an understanding of class as a continual process.

Fieldwork: wave two

On completion of the first interview, I left participants with a disposable camera and instructions to take 15 to 20 photos of 'food-related aspects of their lives'. Visual methods are increasingly being used to study everyday domestic practices (for example, Pink 2004; Pink et al 2015; Meah and Jackson 2016; Waitt and Phillips 2016), and studies into domestic food

Table 1.1: The participants

Pseudonym	Age
Carla	45–54
Charlie	45–54
Des	55–64
Ed	65+
Elizabeth	65+
Fiona	65+
Grace	65+
Gregg	35–44
Harriet	55–64
Helen	55–64
Ian	25–34
Ingrid	25–34
Irene	55–64
Jane	45–54
John	35–44
Julie	35–44
Juliette	35–44
Layla	35–44
Linda	45–54
Mary	35–44
Maya	45–54
Neil	45–54
Peter	25–34
Philip	55–64
Sara	25–34
Steve	35–44
Thomas	65+

practices have generated valuable data via discussions around participant-generated photos (for example, Owen et al 2010; Beagan et al 2015; Harman and Cappellini 2015; Klasson and Ulver 2015; O'Connell and Brannen 2016; Wills et al 2016). I returned some months later with the photos developed for our second interaction. During my second visit, my participants and I discussed their photographs which both acted as reference points and prompts for further discussion and enriched data generated during the first wave of fieldwork around themes of homemade, convenience, feeding families and time management. Echoing Wills et al's observation (2016), most participants recorded aspects of 'front stage' behaviour as opposed to 'backstage' (Goffman 1959). For instance, as Figure 1.1 depicts, most participant-generated images show the final outcomes of what respondents perceived to be positive aspects of their food habits, as opposed to the more hidden aspects of food practices, such as dirty dishes. This lack of 'backstage' could merely suggest a preference to photograph aesthetically pleasing aspects of foods. However, listening to stories about the images generated an additional layer to the data; it became apparent that my participants' understandings of 'homemade' were often expressed via feelings of discomfort around convenience or mass-produced foodstuffs. Ingrid's photo (Figure 1.1) and its accompanying interview excerpt illustrates:

> 'Another standard meal. Fajitas seems to be a regular thing for us as well, lots of vegetables and a bit of leftover … either some chicken but not too much, or leftover meat from a roast dinner goes into fajitas. And shop-bought guacamole there, probably because it was reduced (laughs), not because of any other reason. I wouldn't normally buy that kind of thing unless it was on offer or reduced.' (Ingrid)

Wave two moved beyond accounting for the reflexive ways participants articulated their food-related dispositions and aimed to unpick the taken-for-granted 'practical logic' (Bourdieu and Wacquant 1992: 22) informing approaches to food. To capture the tacit knowledge underpinning food practices and perspectives which are less easy to articulate – the doing as opposed to the narration of practice – wave two research encounters were much more active than the first. I 'hung out' in kitchens to deepen my understanding of the material and sensory contexts in which participants lived their everyday lives. I listened, experienced, and observed participant judgements and knowledge about food and by actually 'being there', I was able to experience how feeding and eating are so entangled with other practices. My conversations with Layla, for example, were continuously interrupted by her two young children who were cutting out pictures for a collage while we chatted. In what Mannay and Morgan (2015) refer to as the 'waiting field', these times of waiting for her to return to our conversation offered opportunities to engage deeper with her experience. Layla often spoke of the challenges of preparing food while caring for her young children. The actual experience of having our conversation interrupted helped enrich and situate her narrative in these everyday moments of competing responsibilities.

In addition, during domestic 'go-alongs' (Kusenbach 2003; Evans 2012), I interviewed participants while following them around the home and kitchen as they cooked or carried out other domestic work. For instance,

Figure 1.1: Ingrid's photo of fajitas

Grace was preparing crème caramels for a dinner party later that evening; Peter, having just returned from work, was cooking dinner for himself and his partner; and Harriet spent most of our second interview ironing. I also invited participants to show me around their kitchens and food-related spaces, providing further observational foci to enrich the verbal data. Following Hurdley's point that 'domestic material cultural displays' (2006: 721) can be used as objects around which to narrate identities, participants shared stories about food-related 'talking points'. For example, cookbooks, the contents of spice racks, or coffee machines became the subject of stories, and these stories then became illustrative of how objects are symbolically and physically integrated into everyday domesticity. Motivated to stay close to the materiality of food, participants and I conducted fridge, freezer, and cupboard 'rummages' (Evans 2012: 44), another important means of identifying participants' embodied relations with food. For instance, participants showed me how they discerned a food's edibility while looking through food storage areas. I was invited to smell an out-of-date yoghurt or take a closer look at packets of herbs which were years past their sell-by-date. Through this process of looking and finding, participants demonstrated the ways in which their practical logic operates via visceral and corporeal assessments of a food's edibility.

Finally, I invited participants to narrate their life stories via the contents of food cupboards. The act of looking often jogged participant memories and became a starting point for the recollection of childhood food practices. These life histories, spoken in situ and narrated with the props of food spaces, generated rich data to compliment the food biographies of our first research interaction. For example, Linda found a bottle of vinegar in her cupboard (Figure 1.2):[3]

Linda: Oh and the vinegar. We always had one of those. I use that for cleaning the windows more than anything else (laughs).

KG: Oh do you? Can I take a photo of that?

Linda: That's kind of reminiscent of childhood. There was always salt and vinegar. What else is there? Oh and Bird's custard of course. Again, I mean that's right at the back which shows how often it gets used. But that reminds me of childhood and I think it's even the same picture.

I now turn to evaluate the steps taken to reflexively analyse the data generated.

Personal reflections and dealing with the data

Data in this book takes many forms (there were 53 transcripts and over 850 research images in all). The process of arriving at the explanations that

---

[3] With participants' consent, I photographed many of my observations. These images are visual representations of my experience of these particular interactions. Similarly, the participant-generated images presented in this book are significant for what they reveal about participants' choice of subject matter, what they identified as important for the research. Thus, the images I present here have not been chosen for their aesthetic qualities, but rather their significance to the analysis that follows. It is also important to note that the inclusion of visual data has required ongoing reflections around anonymity. The use of images has been carefully considered, with some images purposefully excluded and others cropped or blurred to preserve participant anonymity.

Figure 1.2: Researcher photo of a bottle of vinegar Linda found in her cupboard

follow has been open and continually revised. Fieldnotes and researcher photos were integral for keeping track of research understandings. Written immediately after every interview and in other impromptu instances, fieldnotes recorded observations, reflections and emerging interpretations of what was happening in the field. Fieldnotes informed a preliminary analysis conducted after the first wave of interviews which identified themes which would benefit from further investigation in the second wave of fieldwork. Following the completion of fieldwork, I systematically analysed the data in its entirety. Transcripts were analysed vertically and horizontally. This entailed mapping detailed indexed summaries for each interview, which included reflections alongside pasted photographs and excerpts from the transcriptions. These chunks of data were then categorized as belonging to, or being indicative of, themes identified in the initial stages of reviewing the research material. These themes were then compared and connected with similar themes from other interviews, resulting in the empirical abstraction of data into something of theoretical relevance.

It is through drawing on communal language and shared interpretative frameworks that we make sense of experience and communicate to others through verbal and visual representation. All fieldwork occurs in a social space in which both the researcher and participant are actively located (Hammersley and Atkinson 2007). We are implicated and position take in a set of social relations akin to a Bourdieusian field. Most participants appeared relatively comfortable with articulating their attitudes and practices, and no participant seemed uneasy when showing me through the privacy of their kitchen. Partly indicative of the type of respondent who may be more at ease in this kind of situation and partly indicative of our established rapport, the willingness displayed by participants suggests that the nature of my presence was non-intrusive. It is noteworthy that our final interviews felt markedly relaxed, no doubt enabled by the casual sociality of hanging out in their kitchen. We drank tea or coffee, sat at kitchen tables, leant against kitchen benches, and moved around participants' kitchens surrounded by a number of markers, such as family photos, children's drawings, utility bills and medical prescriptions. These all spoke of the intimate details of their lives. As Pink notes, 'doing research in the home is not just about prying behind closed doors, but about entering the space where people work out issues in their private lives for themselves' (2004: 29). This is the environment in which participants shared their stories with me as a visitor. It is important to recognize that the analysis I offer here is generated from my experience of this intimate locality.

In the research moment, my observations were selective, as were the lines of enquiry I pursued. Likewise, participants selectively shared stories, made choices about what to photograph and show me, and above all, actively selected *themselves* for participation (albeit with different degrees of enthusiasm). This of course has consequences for the production of knowledge. Similarly, my role in making class in this research is significant. I brought to each interaction my own class history and position which impacted on my access to and rapport with participants. But while there is no neutral space from which to articulate sociological explanation, it is equally important to abstain from narrating myself into this research as a means to neutralize my subjectivity. On the contrary, this would assume my centrality, resulting, not in the reduction of bias, but in 'eclipsing and de-authorizing the articulations of others' (Skeggs 2002: 312). It *is* important, however, to acknowledge the power dynamics in the research interactions and analysis, and in the wider world. These dynamics implicate and frame both mine and the participants' ways of knowing about food.

To some extent, I was 'studying sideways' (Plsener 2011: 471). That is, the participants and I share a similar class position. At times, participants assumed I shared their classed understandings, which functioned to establish a bond and break down barriers. However, as rightly pointed out by Mellor et al, the idea of 'class matching' is problematic and does not necessarily ensure affinity (2014: 138). Several factors intersect our class identity and experience, which function to locate me as both similar to and different from the participants. For instance, my age, gender, regional identity, and status as a mother impacted on the ways people related to me. However, I refrained from over-identifying with possible shared experiences, in particular my experience as a mother, regardless of its potential to create a sense of solidarity. I felt that to do so ran the risk of eliciting performances of a culturally constructed version of motherhood, which is both restrictive and potentially places boundaries on narratives (Broom et al 2009). But while I was conscious not to explicitly share information relating to my own personal biography, on a number of occasions I shared food knowledge and performed recognition around food. One experience which is absolutely shared by myself and my participants is that we eat. But actually, what became apparent is that we also shared similar classed knowledge about food. The exchange between Thomas and I as we look through his fridge illustrates:

Thomas: (Thomas points to a packet of herbs) That's some ... oh what's that (long pause)?
KG: Coriander.
Thomas: Coriander, thank you (laughs).
KG: Well flat-leaf parsley and coriander, it's always a gamble (laughs).
Thomas: I was going to say parsley, but that's the thing. So that's just hanging around.

The immersive interactions at the centre of this research involved a constant shifting of positions. From these shifting positions, I learnt about the details of my participants' lives and shared and recognized knowledge relating to food. The free-flowing nature of these research conversations suggests that there may be something very particular about food. Had I been looking at middle-classness and other practices – education for example – these conversations may not have been so smooth. Class can be a difficult subject, and some things are presented as more classed than others. But food appears to have allowed conversations to flow around potential obstacles. As one participant said: 'food is a social lubricant'. The apparent ordinariness and everydayness of food invoked a pattern of shareability that made it feel like a safe territory and ostensibly easy to talk about. This is of course indicative of a base line of knowledge that I have as a middle-class researcher and the capital which I brought to each encounter. I am aware of the cultural, classed, and social dynamics that exist around food, and I drew on this awareness methodologically and analytically. Together, the respondents and I drew on common sets of references and shared interpretations and experiences which functioned to establish taken-for-granted and shared knowledge about food and eating. This reciprocation of shared resources both helped overcome the hurdle of positionality and assisted the flow of the conversation. They passed by largely unnoticed in the moment. But that the majority of these interactions were smooth and trouble-free is in itself indicative of the classed ways in which knowledge about food operates at a common-sense level. Together we exhibited a whole series of unproblematized (classed) cultural landmarks around items of food and types of food practices which work to create a good and comfortable domestic setting. Yet, far from denoting bias, these settings show how the public language of food can be a prop to our personal stories signifying the relational and contextual nature of knowledge this research offers.

Book outline

In the following chapter, I explore key perspectives surrounding class, identity, consumption and food. Drawing on Bourdieusian approaches to class and identity, I explore how the middle-class identity is positioned and reproduced as legitimate. I situate the importance of class analysis in relation to everyday eating by engaging with current debates relating to taste and consumption. Exploring the cultural omnivore alongside work pertaining to postmodern ideas of consumption, I ask what constitutes authorized identity and take the position that valued personhood entails the marking of the self with a diverse, yet selective, array of cultural forms. I think through ideas of choice and reflexivity to locate food consumption within increasingly fragmented dynamics of taste. I then use these ideas in conversation with work that focuses on materialities of food consumption to get a closer understanding of the temporally and spatially situated doing of food. Here the concept of domestication is analytically important. Domestication establishes the active ways that objects of consumption are incorporated into the home according to socio-cultural relations which, as the following chapters will show, operate around the valuing of classed individuality. To this end, the importance of gender comes to the fore, specifically, the relationship between classed femininity and the temporality of practices and their associated constraints and priorities. Combined, these theoretical underpinnings provide the foundations from which to explore the empirical stories which unfold in the subsequent chapters.

Working with individual food biographies, Chapter 3 offers a socio-historical framing of participants' self-understandings through food. I start by considering the extent to which participants construct their identity as classed (or not) before juxtaposing these identity performances with participants' food dispositions. Narratives of *not* belonging emerged powerfully across the sample. Participants appeared to distance themselves from being a monolithic product of their upbringings or collective class categories, offering instead a fragmented and reflexive account of their individuality and an orientation towards taste expansion and diversification. While this was recurrently conceptualized in relation to the increased *production* of variety offered by the global marketplace, participants' openness to diversity appeared highly selective. Furthermore, the imagined figure of a working-class mass consumer emerged in these accounts as a point from which to enact differentiation.

Chapter 4 focuses on practice, in particular the material and symbolic ways in which participants chose and restricted the food which crosses the domestic threshold. Starting in one participant's kitchen, I then cast the net further afield to trace the complex processes by which food becomes domesticated. I look towards the consumer marketplace to consider how participants navigate across shopping spaces to select food. In this framing, processed convenience foods clearly emerged as lacking value: they cannot be individually infused with value. Yet data generated from 'hanging out' in the kitchen shows that there were convenience foods in all kitchens and that the dichotomous relationship between convenience and homemade is continuously reworked and contested. Furthermore, accounting for practices highlights the centrality of gender. Female participants were clearly responsible for the day-to-day doings of domestic food, integral to which is the synchronization of multiple time-space paths. I conclude the chapter by reading their justifications about using convenience in relation to broader food narratives in which classed notions of femininity circulate.

Chapter 5 explores how knowledge about food is embodied and reproduced. I begin by taking public health messaging as an example to explore how ideas of self-control operate as 'common-sense' knowledge. Mapping participant journeys from the past to the present, I note the centrality of feminized learning about practices of food provisioning, which is supplemented with accrued culinary capital (such as cookbooks). Together, this appears to produce a strategic disposition to critically select from the diverse foodscape to enact a very particular and culturally shared version of good taste. I then look to the household meal, as the end moment of the domestic sharing of 'good' food, to consider how these frames come together. I especially focus on feeding children to examine how these learnt and accrued knowledges about food unfold across the generations and show how encouraging a disposition to make discerning choices clearly emerges as valued.

Finally, Chapter 6 gathers the key themes of this book to offer concluding remarks pertaining to the ways middle-classness is reproduced and communicated through everyday domestic food practices. In the analysis that follows I hope to show that social boundaries, such as class, operate as a guide to the selection of food. Yet in an era of individualized identities and a neoliberal emphasis on personal choice and responsibility, there is a lack of scrutiny about how access to 'good' foods relies on the possession of multiple forms of capital. One of the effects of overlooking the processes by which good food is accessed is that access becomes dislocated from social divisions such as class and becomes normalized. I aim to redress this by offering a nuanced account of 'good' food and the valued identities configured through its consumption.

2

Class, Consumption and the Domestication of Food

This chapter begins by engaging with debates about class and identity, paying particular attention to the concept of habitus. This permits me to then consider how middle-class identities are positioned as synonymous with authorized ideas of individuality. I then mobilize these conceptual tools in order to evaluate sociology of consumption literature and more specifically the consumption of food. Here, I engage with the cultural omnivore thesis to locate food consumption within increasingly fragmented dynamics of taste. The final section of the chapter engages with literature which accounts for the material and symbolic ways in which food comes to be incorporated into the home. The chapter concludes by focusing on the relationship between time, domestic practice and gender. This provides the foundations from which to consider how eating and feeding others in the domestic sphere relates to classed and gendered performances of authorized identities.

Class and identity matters

In the 1990s, sociology underwent a retreat from class. Materialist approaches to class analysis which focused on the division of labour were increasingly posited as redundant, and the fragmentation associated with post-industrialization meant that traditional understandings of class composition were being transformed. With the apparent decomposition of collective categories came theoretical ideas about reflexive individualism and the argument that structural moorings, such as class, were no longer a relevant category of analysis for investigations of inequality. As Beck argued 'the notion of a class society remains useful only as an image of the past' (1992: 91). Instead, inequality was increasingly understood as an individualized project: 'the *inequality of dealing with insecurity and reflexivity*' (1992: 98; italics original).

In recent years there has been a move to reinstate the importance of class in British sociology by incorporating the interplay between economic, cultural and social resources. For instance, the Great British Class Survey's attempt to drive forward a multidimensional way of thinking about class was met with overwhelming popularity when seven million people clicked on the BBC's 'Class Calculator' within a week of its launch (Savage et al 2015). Clearly, class positioning is a keen point of intrigue to fractions of the British public, but it is also a contentious topic. Class analysis also highlights that class consciousness is not attached to notions of group belongingness in a straightforward way (Savage 2000, 2003). Indeed, in Britain, class carries ideological baggage (Savage et al 2015), and studies find that large numbers of professional people claim a working-class identity when they are objectively middle class (Evans and Mellon 2016; Reay 2017; Friedman et al 2021).

If, as Skeggs suggests, 'class is a discursive, historically specific construction' (1997: 5), then class must be understood in relation to a particular historical context in which theoretical assertions about individualism and fragmentation persist. Thus, to allow for the inclusion of class within neoliberal shifts towards a more individualized form of sociality, my primary focus here is on how class is experienced and understood at an individual level: to the *individualization* of class. This provides an ideal point of departure from which to think about class as a lived identity, as something which is subjectively experienced in relation to objective structures, and therefore allows for the complexities of class to be understood alongside other divisions, such as gender. As several feminist scholars have argued, focusing on experiences, emotions, and attitudes extends the concept of class to account for the social and cultural frameworks within which individuals mediate their lives (see for example, Skeggs 1997; Reay 1998, 2005; Lawler 1999). As Reay emphasizes, 'class is always lived on a conscious and unconscious level' (2005: 912) through everyday practices. Attending to everyday practices then lays bare the relationship between social position and identity because practices act as a lens through which to see the lived and situated relations of class. That is, practices can be analysed as both products and reactions to the structuring processes at work. Furthermore, food plays a unique role in this framing because of the way it is embodied: 'what we eat is literally incorporated into our bodies' (Beagan et al 2015: 17), and yet our experience of food is simultaneously embedded in socio-cultural relations. To elaborate on this further, I turn to Bourdieu's concept of habitus as a frame of reference to explain how practices and dispositions reflect the ways in which class is both embedded in the self and is constitutive of social relations (Lawler 2004).

Habitus, capital, field and practice

Bourdieu's concept of habitus enables us to consider how social relations come to be embodied as practical knowledge which itself is related to an individual's position within a field of socially distributed resources (Wacquant

2013). Habitus refers to an (often unconscious) practical logic giving rise to sets of dispositions (perceptions and practices) within hierarchically structured fields. Fields can be defined as a particular social setting, as well as a broader and abstract space, where class dynamics occur (Silva 2005); the stimuli of fields are structured according to the exchange and conversion of capital. Thus, for Bourdieu, the field is the site of power struggles. For example, the consumer marketplace can be conceptualized as a field because it is a hierarchically structured space where consumption occurs. The valuing of and access to goods in the field of consumption is related to a person's possession of capital. For Bourdieu (1984), there are three main types of capital: economic capital (financial resources), social capital (resources accrued from belonging to particular social networks) and cultural capital (forms of knowledge and competence). Bourdieu's argument is that the likelihood of accruing capital, as well as the ability to mark forms of capital as legitimate, is dependent on an individual's position in the field. An individual's position in the field, as well as their future trajectory, depends on the volume and composition of the different types of capital they inherit.

The concepts of habitus, field and capital help unpack the relationship between food and class because the classed positions we encounter mark our bodies and inform practice. Habitus is embodied and adjusted according to an individual's position and trajectory within and between fields (Bourdieu 1990a; 1990b). Being unconscious and tending to concur with its conditions of production, habitus captures social continuity. Referring to the imprint of history which lies within an individual, it is 'embodied history, internalized as second nature and so forgotten as history' (Bourdieu 1990b: 56). Everyday practice is thus accepted as common-sense and self-evident. To this end, habitus is useful for considering how eating is a function of embodied class position while at the same time essentialized as a personal attribute. It provides a *relational* way to understand how class informs our access to food, as well as how we are individually positioned through our food choices.

Contrary to its critics (for example, Jenkins 1982), habitus is not passively inscribed on the Bourdieusian body. Rather, it is the result of a practical and mediating relationship between objective structures and everyday action, where the social world is understood through categories constructed by previous experience. These categories, or dispositions, are durable and generative but are reflexively realized. Habitus 'is an *open system of dispositions* that is constantly subjected to experiences, and therefore constantly affected by them' (Bourdieu and Wacquant 1992: 133; italics original). It thus refers to an active, not passive, set of dispositions which through interaction with the field can generate subjective motivating structures that can override an individual's inherited attitudes and knowledges (McNay 2008). The importance of our trajectory across and within fields is fundamental for this analysis because it captures the extent to which learnt food dispositions change from place-to-place and from time-to-time but are nonetheless related to a 'feel for the game' (Bourdieu 1990a: 63). Paying attention to an individual's feel for the game encapsulates how habitus is informed by an individual's history but adapted in relation to their shifting positions in fields. It thus opens up the concept of class as something which is both a historical formation and individually realized.

Class, then, is embedded in personal history but is continually disrupted as people move across class categories. Social mobility was given little empirical attention by Bourdieu aside from his reflections about his own experiences of upward social mobility (Lawler 1999; Friedman 2015; Friedman and Savage 2018). Yet paying attention to the experience of social mobility is an ideal way to uncover the relationship between habitus and individual experience of social change. Studies have established the ambiguous and often painful ways in which the upwardly mobile experience a dissonance between their origin and destination tastes and practices (Lawler 1999; Reay et al 2009; Friedman 2012, 2015; Reay 2013, 2018; Mallman 2018), yet few have explored how food practices relate to life stages and shifting class positions. Scholars have called for future research to investigate the relationship between families and food across the life course, especially during critical moments of transition (Jackson 2009). For instance, McKenzie and Watts (2020) reveal how eating patterns can be modified in response to transitions and turning points within the life course, suggesting further research is needed to explore how class features in these changing social structures. Indeed, Beagan et al (2015) find that with changing class positions, childhood food practices are often misaligned with new economic and social circumstances. With this in mind, the concept of habitus is a way to understand change and continuity as being related to both the accrual of capital *and* categories of perception constructed by history and experience.

Classed identities then, cannot be read as *fixed* to an objective position, rather they are processual and realized through practices which themselves (re)produce social relations. It is in this respect that the practices of those situated in dominant class positions can be analysed as an indication of the role that structures play in assigning and reproducing value to practices. The legitimization of capital entails the conversion of objective differences between cultural objects, for instance food, into recognizable distinctions based on the status benefits they provide: '[a]ny difference that is recognized, accepted as legitimate, functions by that very fact as a symbolic capital providing a profit of distinction' (Wacquant 2013: 297). For Bourdieu (1991), the mobilization of forms of capital into symbolic capital entails its reproduction as legitimate through misrecognition. That is, the process through which value is reproduced is misrecognized as natural, thus concealing the power of those who can legitimize cultural capital. It is in this way that middle-class practices become normalized – access to high volumes of capital yields more opportunities to enact taste distinctions through legitimization. Investigations into the middle-class habitus, then, can push against this process and problematize the reproduction and normalization of 'standards of excellence' (Warde 2014: 291) relating to food.

Bourdieu has been criticized for abandoning the concepts of field and practice from the theoretical reasonings which form the basis of his study in *Distinction* (1984), largely due to his overreliance on habitus (Warde 2004, 2008; Bennett 2007). Here I foreground practice, and in so doing, highlight how everyday food practices can sometimes be misaligned with habitus and its associated preferences. As Warde (2004) rightly points out, not all practices are reducible to the strategic pursuit of capital. Indeed, eating is necessary to survive, and paying attention to the intimacy of the domestic sphere shows how practices are not always aligned with preference and taste, which I will go on to explore in Chapter 4. However, paying attention to practices which are valued and deemed appropriate for the pursuit of capital is important for understanding the socially divisive ways that legitimate food choices are (mis)recognized. It is on this note that I move to establish the conceptual importance of focusing on the middle classes. In the following section I position food as a means for culture and class to meet on the body and argue that particular ways of eating *are* reducible to the strategic pursuit of middle-classed capital, albeit in complex ways.

The middle classes: valued identities

I have so far argued that class is individualized. As Savage writes, 'individualisation involves making claims to social distinction through a process of defining oneself in relation to the other' (2000: 105–106). So let us now consider the relationship between class and individualism, the notion that identities are the result of individual and reflexive self-making. Under the rhetoric of neoliberalism, politics and social self-understandings have been reshaped by discourses of individualism. Reflexive choice is central to neoliberalism and, to use the words of Tyler, a 'normative middle-class self is the neoliberal subject *par excellence*' (2015: 500; italics original). Considering this, I follow claims that individualism universalizes middle-class experience (Savage 2000; Skeggs 2004a) by working on the assumption that everyone can, and should, have access to (structural) resources which enable self-making (Skeggs 2005). Nonetheless, *because* reflexive individualism resonates with middle-class experience and is fundamental in the social construction of valued personhood (Skeggs 2004a), it is relevant for investigations into middle-class identities as I will go on to explore.

One of the central objectives of this book is to address class reproduction. My argument is that class reproduction centres on the valuing and legitimization of middle-class personhood and that class is made and reproduced through individual selves responsible for living up to (classed) norms. There is a lack of research which takes the middle classes as its primary focus. Rather, the middle classes appear in research as a background against which 'othered' practices are contrasted and the normal against which other groups are measured (Lawler 2011; Allen 2014; Loveday 2015). But research into middle-class practice is important because it sheds light on how systems of knowledge and representation assign importance to those perspectives which can be heard, rendering others invisible. As Savage (2003, 2015) suggests, paying attention to the activities of the advantaged positions them as open to critique, therefore making it possible to identify widening forms of inequality. To this end, focusing on the claims to normality associated with the middle-class identity provides a route into legitimate culture. It is therefore imperative to scrutinize dominant norms which position 'good' food alongside the middle classes, while at the same time presenting food as inherently 'classless' (Johnston et al 2011). To conceptualize this further, I now turn to ideas of access and exclusion to expand on the ways in which middle-class personhood has become shorthand for the individual.

From this I want to establish how both individualism as well as the concept of habitus (even though it recognizes that the self is produced in conditions not entirely of its own making) rely on ideas of investment and self-interest (Skeggs 2011). Here, Skeggs significantly reminds us that 'proper personhood' is a resource in itself and constituted through exclusion. That is, valued personhood is broadly understood in relation to that which it is not: the working classes defined through their distance from individuality (the masses) and positioned as improper (through their lack). Following this understanding, then, is the idea that the working classes are constituted as the other to a middle-class norm. For instance, interventionist policies which use terms such as 'raising achievement' or 'widening participation' position working-class people as not knowing, not valuing, not doing, and not wanting the 'right' things. This does little more than fix 'working-classness' as something from which one must endeavour to 'escape' in order to accrue value to oneself (Lawler 1999, 2014; Reay 2005; Allen 2014; Shildrick 2018). Investing in the self through access to resources is a central way in which middle-class identities are formed. Yet the consequence of this is the marginalization and devaluing of the working classes.

The positioning of working-class personhood as devoid of value has a long history. A number of studies have highlighted that the positioning of the middle-class habitus as desirable entails the marking of working-class identities and practices as negative (see for example, Skeggs 1997; 2004b; 2005; Lawler 2004, 2005, 2011; Reay 2005, 2017; Tyler 2008; Gidley and Rooke 2010; Jackson and Benson 2014; Reay et al 2011;). Central to these studies is the finding that the working classes are axiomatically marked as pathologically failing to reflexively organize socially valued resources to invest in middle-class identities. The consequences of class are essentialized and individualized. For instance, Lawler's (2018) analysis of British government reports draws our attention to the individualized political rhetoric about social mobility. She notes that these reports focus on ensuring the socially immobile have the right skillset and character to be successful individuals. The emphasis is on accumulating capital in order to become a person of value. Yet none of the government reports in her study consider *how* cultural capital comes to be valued in the first place.

Furthermore, the valueless person is positioned as *refusing* to accrue value to themselves. Reay argues that the working classes are often blamed for their lack of social mobility: 'they are presented either as "decent and hardworking"– those who are engaged in trying to become middle class – or else as failures who are either not aspiring enough or not making sufficient effort to be viewed as successful individuals' (2017: 13). The media, of course, offers countless examples. Terms such as 'benefits mum' or 'chav' (Tyler 2015) refer not to a collective working-class other, but to individuals who are to blame for their diminished resources. Skeggs and Wood's (2008) research into reality television shows how working-class participants are pathologized for being individually responsible for their lack of self-investment and lack of access to the cultural capital required for valued self-production. This positioning makes them ripe for transformation by middle-class professionals, and the viewer is invited to adopt the subject position that accruing middle-class value to oneself is a moral imperative. This is classed because the production of proper personhood requires both recognition of and access to legitimate capital. What these examples show is that, as Loveday (2015) suggests, there is a public narrative which endorses a need to 'fix' the working classes by making them like their middle-class counterparts.

Following Skeggs (2004a), I argue that to understand how class is reproduced, it is necessary to significantly extend class analysis beyond the exchange-value of capital and focus instead on those perspectives which accord objects with value, thus making them exchangeable. This means looking beyond the strategic investment of capital to account for exclusion and access, because to ignore exclusion and access reproduces the properties of an exchange-value self as having value. Moreover, linking action only to the strategic pursuit of capital offers no explanation of how those who occupy valueless positions in social space are denied access to the fields of exchange wherein they are able to convert, accrue or generate legitimate value to themselves (Skeggs 2004b; 2011). For instance, the working-class women in Skeggs' seminal study (1997) exchanged resources and attached legitimacy to their practices not as a means of accruing future value for themselves, but to gain respectability and defend themselves against misrecognition.

Skeggs shows how class is made through exclusion; that not everyone is encapsulated in Bourdieu's depiction of social space, and that habitus fails to draw our attention to how those who are denied access to the field can accrue value for themselves. Nevertheless, Bourdieu's concepts are useful here because they highlight the strategic ways that middle-class boundary-marking is conducted and therefore the ways in which the *middle classes* are made. Studies have noted that the middle classes share a strong commitment to their social reproduction, particularly through their possession of cultural capital. For instance, the systematic ways in which middle-class families ensure that their children gain access to the 'right' schools and universities are well documented as being a central means of intergenerational reproduction of cultural capital (Reay 1998, 2017; Ball 2003; Crozier et al 2008; Reay et al 2011). Employing habitus to understand how people are distributed in classed space and how this in turn informs their trajectory through food moments lays bare the systems of exchange which exclude certain people by positioning them as valueless subjects. By focusing on the ways in which class dissolves into individualized identities, the performance of 'good' food can be theorized through broader inequalities, rather than individualized notions of effort and aspiration. With this in mind, I now turn to evaluating sociology of consumption literature which provides a starting point from which to consider what constitutes 'good' food and the processes by which it comes to be named as such. I engage with work pertaining to postmodern ideas of consumption in order to situate food consumption within a Bourdieusian hierarchical field. In so doing, I think through ideas of choice and reflexivity alongside the increasingly fragmented taste hierarchy and argue that ways of consuming are classed.

The field of consumption

There is widespread agreement about the importance of consumption in contemporary Britain (Warde 2017), and there is a growing body of literature which, taking the consumption of food as its primary focus, aims to describe and uncover the minutiae of consumers' relationships with existing food hierarchies. For instance, research conducted by Johnston and colleagues in Canada establishes that while economic and cultural capital shape access to ethical food discourses, shoppers who are wealthy in capital are consistently positioned as more reflexive and intellectually superior to their low-income counterparts (Johnston and Szabo 2011; Johnston et al 2012). These insights not only draw our attention to a stratified food system, but also remind us of the rhetoric of individual choice in consumerism.

With the flourishing of consumption studies, the somewhat pervasive figure of the individualized consumer has emerged as a symbolic representation of taste and lifestyle. Much of this stems from the highly influential work of Bauman, Beck and Giddens who argue that in reflexive modernity, consumption (of goods, practices and knowledge) is central to the construction and communication of identity. Importantly, reflexive consumption is understood as the means by which identity comes to be *realized* on individual bodies. For instance, Giddens argued that 'the body, like the self, becomes a site of interaction, appropriation and reappropriation, linking reflexively organized processes and systematically ordered expert knowledge' (1991: 218). To reiterate my earlier point, placing theoretical emphasis on mobile and reflexive selves carved out through consumption situates practice as the outcome of individual reflexive, albeit 'precarious freedoms' (Beck and Beck-Gernsheim 2009: 13). For Bauman (2009), the freedom of choice and personal responsibility implied through consumerism in 'liquid modernity' (the constant and restless shifting of social relationships) leads to anxiety. It also produces a spectre of failed consumers: those without either the material or cultural resources to even 'have' an identity in a consumerized world. In relation to this, it is useful here to explore Warde's (1994) focus on the cultural and social locatedness of consumer anxiety and reflexivity. Warde argues that anxiety about consumption is avoided through group identification and that the dynamics of consumption are related to social attributes. Furthermore, if consumerism constructs identity and is inherently anxiety-provoking then one would expect high levels of anxiety among affluent consumers, since they have a greater choice of 'identity' options and a greater investment in identity construction via (legitimized) aesthetic display: 'members of these groups would suffer the highest potential personal embarrassment from contravening the standards of acceptable taste through the making of inappropriate choices' (1994: 893). They are, however, less likely to make mistakes. This is because they are supported through sharing legitimated style (social capital), access to knowledge (cultural capital) and economic resources and having a clear sense of the rules.

Attending to the notion of choice is important here since food is selected from the consumer marketplace within which the rhetoric of individual choice circulates. Much research into food consumption has drawn our attention to the 'menu pluralism' (Beardsworth and Keil 1992) offered in the consumer marketplace as a result of globalization and mass production. Mennell's (1985) 40-year-old study argued that this increase in variety has resulted in the diminishing of social contrasts between classes. This claim has since been widely refuted (see Warde 1997 for a full discussion), not least for its correlation of production of variety with consumption of variety. Nonetheless, there still remains an idea, particularly in the public imagination, that globalization has eroded traditional boundaries, replacing relatively fixed socially recognized criteria with the free play of individual choice (Fischler 1988; Crouch and O'Neil 2000). There is, however, little evidence of what these 'traditional' foodways of the past looked like in the first place.

Warde (1997) suggests that imagined food traditions are invented as a way to negotiate a tension around individual choice. He argues that the process of *selection* must be understood in relation to broader consumer frameworks which centralize consumption as a symbolic communication of identity. Warde's comparison of food magazines from 1968 and 1992 showed that in the 1960s an appeal to foreign cuisine became commonplace, but by the 1990s foreign cuisine was so commonplace that its novel appeal had declined in what he refers to as 'the routinization of the exotic' (1997: 61). In other words, the global marketplace was so awash with variety that it had now become the norm. Now over 25 years old, Warde's oft-cited text has been an important counterargument to theorizing consumption as a form of personal symbolic communication because he emphasizes the social locatedness of consumption and its role in maintaining social relationships. He outlines that the food choices individuals make within routinized variety operate within four antinomies: novelty and tradition, health and indulgence, economy and extravagance, and convenience and care. These antonyms are socially and historically located and are used to make sense of contradictory public narratives about food selection. For instance, the opposition of health and indulgence reflects contradictory social concerns about excess, self-surveillance, and resistance of abundance. Importantly, since the ideology of individual choice in consumerism offers little guidance around diversity, the ways in which consumers navigate these contradictory evaluations is *read* as reflecting individual identities.

The chapters that follow extend Warde's insights by offering contemporary data about the nuanced ways that the analytical antinomies he identifies play out in practice. For instance, the public narrative of austerity draws our attention to the economy and extravagance antonym in which practices of thrift could be attempts to address. And yet, Cappellini and Parsons (2013) show how thrift practices are not just a reaction to austerity but reflect a symbolic (and moral) relationship with material goods. Furthermore, important to explore is how class operates in subtle ways around the valuing of choices in the negotiation of these antonyms. For instance, if the quest for novel or exotic cuisines co-exists alongside a quest for security which can be found through the valuing of 'traditional' foods, then I would argue that class exists in the successful balancing of the two opposing ways of consuming. Likewise, the ways in which ideas about caregiving through food are understood to be compromised using convenience foods relates to classed and gendered ideas about appropriate caregiving. I will develop this point about the classed and gendered nature of the care and convenience antonym later in the chapter when I consider the temporalities of everyday food provisioning. Following Meah and Jackson (2017), while at the level of abstraction these antonyms are in polar opposition, paying attention to everyday practice can delineate the ways in which these oppositions can be reconciled, even if in tension. I would also point out that these antonyms are themselves classed. Their oppositional positioning relates to particular classed perspectives about foods and ways of eating, and how the navigation of these antonyms can be socially valued relates to legitimized ideas of taste and distinction. Socially valued navigation centres on the successful presentation of individual choice. This is performed through the critical discernment of *appropriate* food and food practices. To elaborate on this further, I now look towards the concepts of taste and distinction.

The boundaries of taste and distinction

Bourdieu's work *Distinction* (1984) provides a useful framework for understanding the central role that taste and distinction play not only in representing but also in demarcating class boundaries. Based on ethnographic research conducted in Paris, the study aligns taste with classed dispositions, rather than individual preference and choice. Bourdieu argues that 'tastes of luxury' (an inclination for aesthetic presentation, for instance speciality foods) are defined through their distance, or distinction, from 'tastes of necessity' (an inclination for function over form, for instance economical foods):

> The true basis of the differences found in the area of consumption, and far beyond it, is the opposition between the tastes of luxury (or freedom) and the tastes of necessity. The former are the tastes of individuals who are the product of material conditions of existence defined by distance from necessity, by the freedoms or facilities stemming from possession of capital; the latter express, precisely in their adjustment, the necessities of which they are the product. (Bourdieu 1984: 177)

His point is that 'tastes of luxury', belonging to the privileged classes, are legitimized as the antithesis to 'tastes of necessity'. Hence, food tastes carry social stakes, not least that they can be made and mobilized as a symbolic marker for reproducing class distinction. Taste reflects and maintains status and distance from other classes and class fractions. Taste is 'a class culture turned into nature, that is, *embodied*, [and] helps to shape the class body' (1984: 190; italics original). Through being well-positioned in the field, middle-class taste is legitimized and valued and therefore regarded as the criteria for normality. Afterall, with the possession of capital comes the capacity to draw boundaries.

Bourdieu's theory of distinction has been criticized for being a rigid and unreflexive model about cultural preferences, particularly in their contemporary forms (Bennett 2007; Ollivier 2008; Warde 2008; Daloz 2011). The fast-moving pace of commodification means that there is an increase of cultural forms in circulation. This is not to suggest that Bourdieu's toolkit is redundant, however. Clearly the British middle classes are quite different from the Parisian bourgeoisie studied by Bourdieu in the 1960s, but resource-based food differentiations persist. For instance, in their correspondence analysis of the relationship between household food consumption and class, Atkinson and Deeming (2015) found that economic and cultural capital influenced household food expenditure and preferences. Participants with rich stocks of capital were found to be more likely to emphasize quality, taste, health, and ethics in relation to their food habits. Similarly, Beagan et al's qualitative study found that Bourdieu's findings are still relevant to food consumption. They argue that while elite tastes have changed, they are still 'distinct, enjoying a high degree of social legitimacy and providing a significant means to distinguish class' (2015: 241). To understand fully how cultural capital can be transformed to enhance the status of its bearer, contemporary understandings of taste ought to focus, not on fixed hierarchies, but on the relationship between dominant capital, tacit knowledge, and choice. As I will now go on to argue, the possession of capital facilitates both the confidence to pursue diversity, as well as the successful conversion of cultural selections into legitimized taste. To this end, as Warde (2017) points out, engaging with the notion of legitimate culture is critical.

In contemporary culture, the boundaries of taste are continuously redrawn, meaning that high, middle and popular culture are up for grabs as symbolic resources to achieve distinction. At face value, engaging with variety could be understood as evidence for an increase in individual autonomy and a decrease in social and cultural hierarchies: the democratization of the cultural field (Warde et al 2008). But the ability, and inclination, to reflexively 'choose' from the array of cultural forms is socially located as we will go on to explore via a discussion of the cultural omnivore thesis, which in recent years has received much attention in the sociology of consumption.

The cultural omnivore

The term cultural omnivore was coined by Peterson (1992) to describe the broad taste profiles of those who cross hierarchical boundaries of high and low culture. It has since become a powerful and important framework in theories of taste and consumption. Peterson's study, based in the United States, posited that theories of taste which rely on an elite-to-mass hierarchy are inadequate and instead identified the emergence of the omnivore as denoting distinction. Since Peterson's observations, several studies have demonstrated that rather than exclusively operating around highbrow tastes, distinction is now attached to variety and breadth of cultural consumption (Warde et al 1999; Emmison 2003; Warde et al 2008; Bennett et al 2009; Warde and Gayo-Cal 2009; Smith Maguire 2018; Yalvaç and Hazir 2021). The crux of the argument is not that the 'omnivore likes everything *indiscriminately*. Rather, it signifies an *openness* to appreciating everything' (Peterson and

Kern 1996: 904; italics original). Omnivorous consumption has come to be associated with those in privileged classed positions because it requires high levels of capital to cross taste boundaries and critically engage with a variety of cultural forms (Warde et al 1999; Oleschuk 2017). The empirical validity of the omnivore thesis is not without criticisms. Ollivier (2008) suggests that the omnivore thesis is popular because it resonates with middle-class experience. This is especially so, since much research uses existing class discourses about what is desirable and undesirable, thus reproducing the taste hierarchy. For instance, through their openness to 'lowbrow' foods, the Turkish middle-class participants in Yalvaç and Hazir's study (2021) understood their broad tastes in hierarchical class terms. But by opening up the taste hierarchy, Ollivier (2008) found that 'lowbrows' are not 'closed' but are as open and curious as their 'highbrow' counterparts, albeit to domains which are not traditionally associated with high culture. Ollivier's working-class participants expressed openness and a desire to learn about technical or practical forms which are useful in everyday life, such as using new tools or trying new sports. These domains, however, have less symbolic value, meaning that 'lowbrows' are unlikely to be recognized as cultural omnivores in the same sense as someone who has the right composition and amount of symbolic and material resources.

Other research has highlighted the prevalence of omnivorous taste profiles in the socially mobile (Peterson and Kern 1996; Friedman 2012; Daenekindt and Roose 2014; Coulangeon 2015). This is because taste profiles of the upwardly mobile include both their origin tastes and destination tastes, thus leading us to question whether boundary-crossing is entirely to do with markers of status. Yet to this Friedman's (2012) research adds that the omnivorousness of the upwardly mobile is more than a cumulative result of individual life trajectories. Through life history interviews, Friedman established that for the upwardly mobile their combined taste portfolios left them unsure of their cultural identity. They lacked the learnt disposition to 'naturalise' their tastes as legitimate, especially the tastes of their childhoods, and consequently they were more 'culturally homeless' than cultural omnivores. The addition of qualitative approaches then is important for deepening our understanding of the consumption of diversity. Much criticism has been levied at the overreliance of the omnivore thesis on quantitative methods (Warde et al 2008; Warde and Gayo-Cal 2009; Hanquinet 2017). Critics primarily argue that quantitative research leaves unanalysed the dynamic meanings of omnivorousness arguing for a need to shift the focus away from statistically measuring how much and what forms are consumed to instead examining people's relationships to both existing and emerging cultural forms and how they are consumed (Hanquinet 2017). To this end, engaging with the omnivore thesis through qualitative research fosters an understanding about how omnivores make sense of their eclectic tastes, highlights the tensions involved in the traversing of hierarchies of taste and, in turn, allows for closer scrutiny of the relationship between legitimate foods and power.

Emmison notes that it is of strategic importance to be flexible and mobile in this complex and fluid era but the 'desire *and* the ability to participate in different social and cultural worlds, are far from universally distributed' (2003: 227; italics original). In other words, the middle classes can make omnivorousness work for them because through access to recourses they can utilize a diverse taste portfolio to increase their exchange-value. Probing an individual's relationship with food, enables questions to be asked about the extent to which omnivorousness operates around inclusion and openness, and the extent to which openness itself is classed. Indeed, Warde et al (2008) found that there are limits to the omnivore's openness and that omnivore dislikes were heavily orientated towards non-legitimate cultural genres, such as reality television and fast food. Much like Bourdieu's insights, for the omnivore distance is pivotal to processes of discernment. This works to keep the classed taste hierarchy intact because uniqueness is coded as such through its differentiation to sameness and mass. To further engage with this theoretical debate, I now turn to consider omnivorousness in relation to food.

Omnivorousness and authenticity: from common to cool

There is an emergent body of literature which shows how openness to food which crosses taste boundaries acts as a culturally and symbolically important means of distinction. Some of this literature focuses on gourmet or 'foodie' culture (for example, Johnston and Baumann 2007, 2014; Oleschuk 2017). For instance, in their examination of American gourmet food magazines, Johnston and Baumann (2014) reveal how conflicting ideologies of democracy and distinction play out through notions of exoticism and authenticity within 'foodie' culture. On the one hand, populism frames omnivorousness through recourse to inclusiveness. On the other hand, there is an obscured ideology of distinction which authorizes a narrow range of food. This 'openness' is highly selective, and it is particularly around notions of authenticity which certain foods are legitimized. The notion of authenticity increasingly dominates the marketplace. Ideas about authenticity circulate in trends for local foods, ethnic and exotic foods, and gourmet, speciality and artisanal foods. But while the fragmentation of formal boundaries of good and bad taste positions food as a 'classless terrain' (Johnston and Baumann 2014: 158), a tension is apparent in the field of food consumption wherein values around what constitutes authentic, or 'good' and 'proper', food compete. This is evident in the juxtaposition of 'kitsch' foods alongside gourmet foods or in trends to move away from the formalities associated with silver-service in the restaurant industry.

Similarly, Smith Maguire (2018) looks at representation of Old and New World Wines in specialist wine magazines. Like Johnston and Baumann (2014), Smith Maguire notes that wines are presented as democratically equal, but at the same time a 'taste for the particular' (2018: 15) is made explicit in the choice-making process. Smith Maguire also argues that choice is legitimized by invoking ideas about authenticity, offered as such through frames of personal connection, geographic specificity and tradition. Thus, 'authenticity is not just something that is but also something that is done' (Askegaard and Brogård 2016: 19). Social recognition rests on the ability to competently navigate conflicting frames of omnivorousness by attaching ideas of authenticity to foods. By paying attention to an individual's relationship to foods and the ways they navigate the taste hierarchy, it is possible to understand how certain foods can be repositioned and accorded status. To use the words of Bourdieu: 'nothing is more distinctive, more distinguished, than the capacity to confer aesthetic status on objects that are banal or even "common"' (1984: 5).

For Spracklen, 'the morality of authenticity elides smoothly into a Western, middle-class sensibility of culture: the authentic is good because it runs counter to the homogenising tendencies of globalisation, because it encourages diversity, respect and cultural heterogeneity' (2011: 102). Spracklen and colleagues draw on their research into real ale to argue that the urban, bourgeois classes' taste for real ale operates around ideas of authenticity and localism. It is a means of distinction from the 'lagerisation of the mainstream' (2013: 317), whereby lager is designated as a low-status class of beer. Likewise, Kierans and Heaney show how the traditional Liverpudlian working-class dish Scouse has been repositioned as a marker for distinction through recourse to authenticity. Importantly, it is not that authenticity is inherent in food itself, but food 'acquires its authenticity from the routines and practices which underpin it, bestowing some quintessential character and forming part of what can be verified as native, local, indigenous' (2010: 111). But if, as Zukin argues in relation to gentrification, 'we can only see spaces as authentic from outside of them' (2008: 728), then consumers of authenticity are united in their shared vantage point of distance. Served from the working-class kitchen to the working-class family, Scouse is not up for grabs as a form of distinction, nor is it positioned as 'authentic'. Such families cannot verify Scouse as having symbolic value because they have insufficient dominant capital to authorize its conversion into a valued authentic dish. 'Authenticity' then is a social and cultural classed construction, ironically significant in the field of consumerism. It operates through a play of difference between autonomy to encounter 'authentic goods' and mass consumption. To consume 'authentic' goods and reappropriate them as legitimate requires the mobility which comes with possession of capital. What is more, as Anguelovski (2015) notes, the gentrification of 'authentic' foods is often coupled with a price inflation resulting in the exclusion of groups who traditionally bought or made them.

Following Skeggs (2004a), I argue that uncovering how positioning, movement, and exclusion are generated is central to understanding class inequalities. There is a classed skill involved in connecting with and appropriating particular cultural selections as a marker for distinction. At the same time, the mobility involved in encountering multiple forms entails fixing the other in a position of exclusion, as a point from which the mobile self can enact selective distance. A number of scholars discuss how emotions of disgust in relation to the working-class other function to position the middle-class self (for example Lawler 2005; Skeggs 2005; Tyler 2008; Gidley and Rooke 2010). Disgust is a powerful, visceral emotion generated by ambivalence and proximity. To borrow Probyn's words, it 'seems to turn on proximity, sight and the closeness of smell and touch: the over-whelming horror that the disgusting object will engulf us' (2000: 131). Since openness to diversity is culturally valued, the boundaries of good and bad taste are ambivalent, resulting in the distorted proximity of good and bad. But while distinction rests on a form of individualism which marks an identity as unique, it nevertheless relies on a shared understanding of taste and distaste. Afterall, the successful marking of distinction through omnivorous consumption rests on universalizing a disposition belonging to a particular (middle-class) location.

For Lawler (2005), middle-classness *relies* on the expulsion of perceived working-classness. Likewise, Skeggs argues, class disgust 'provides collective reassurance that we are not alone in our judgement of the disgusting object, generating consensus and authorization for middle-class standards, maintaining the symbolic order' (2005: 970). Attached to taste is the antithesis of distaste, and if disgust hangs on proximity then those perceived as lacking taste need to be rendered disgusting in order to maintain the opposition. There is a lack of research which specifically explores how emotions of disgust operate in relation to food practices and classed identities. But paying attention to disgust, even if articulated in the subtlest of ways, can reveal how identities entail the marking of classed, albeit individualized, boundaries in relation to an other. In this way, foods and ways of eating which are positioned as disgusting are not just deemed unworthy of investment but signify a potential devaluing and contamination of the habitus. This could be particularly relevant to the omnivore since disgust occurs as a response to being in the realm of uneasy categories. Accounting for disgust therefore can reveal the tacit knowledge which positions certain foods and ways of consuming as having no value and therefore those which need to be repelled in order to protect the self's interests. As Bourdieu suggests, 'tastes are no doubt first and foremost distastes, disgust provoked by horror or visceral intolerance ("sick-making") of the tastes of others' (1984: 56).

I have thus far focused on the connections between consumption and class to argue that there is a relationship between positionality and the ability to engage in practices of distinction through food. To this end, I have reworked theories of individualization and reflexivity, which, while they fall short in acknowledging the importance of social divisions such as class, are important for identifying the fractured nature of contemporary society and its individualizing tropes. From this, I take the position that class analysis needs to examine how particular modes of individualization are related to class and that valued personhood entails the marking of the self with a diverse, yet selective, array of cultural forms. To complete the foundations of the empirical chapters that follow, the final section of this chapter unpicks the conditions in which food, as a material object, comes to be transformed into something which can be read as a cultural marker for class.

Materialities of food

Accounting for the material–social processes through which people adopt domestic feeding practices and preferences can point towards the social and cultural environment which shapes ideas about which foods are edible in the home. In this section, I engage with literature and debate about the role of food in the making of the home to offer insights about how class emerges in the material processes of domestic food practices.

Home and domestication

Cultural geography studies have sought to draw attention to how the concept of home refers to the multidimensional ways in which social relationships interact with place (Mallett 2004; Blunt 2005; Pink et al 2015). In this context, the home can be conceptualized as a 'place-event', a material and sensory context, which is lived, continually changing and constituted through its relation to everyday activity (Pink et al 2015). This extends beyond the physical boundaries of the home. For instance, the spatial design of the home reflects and reproduces cultural and historical ideas about forms of sociality associated with domesticity (Blunt 2005). This can be seen in the contemporary kitchen which has evolved from a backstage setting for mundane food work to a space for living (Hand and Shove 2004; Hand et al 2007; Meah 2016).

Each home operates as a unique site of consumption, since the meanings ascribed to goods are negotiated between those who live there and the wider world. Hurdley's (2006) research into mantelpiece displays denotes this intersection of the social and the personal. Hurdley's participants engaged in wider frameworks of social meanings to represent domestic relationships and enact their identities through narratives about mantelpiece displays. In the same way, domestic food processes which (re)produce the home are related to external, as well as internal, social frameworks. Domestic ways of doing are connected to a wider symbolic order associated with notions of class and gender for example. In light of this, I look beyond the physical boundaries of the home to account for the ways in which individuals negotiate external socio-spatial relations in their 'doing' of home. This permits me in turn to now address the concept of domestication to embed domestic food practices in a wider social framework. Domestication is 'a process of bringing things home – machines and ideas, values and information – which always involves the crossing of boundaries: above all those between the public and private, and between proximity and distance, is a process which also involves their constant renegotiation' (Silverstone 2005: 233). Encapsulating how things external to a private space can be appropriated through domestic processes, domestication blurs the public/private dichotomy by delineating the ways in which global processes are actively mediated, negotiated, and remade through their symbolic and physical integration into the everyday. Much of the domestication literature focuses on technology and the conflicting processes by which it becomes mundane and ordinary in everyday domestic life (for example, Silverstone and Haddon 1996; Haddon 2018). Here, domestication refers to 'a set of practices (appropriation, objectification, incorporation, adaptation and conversion) to describe the introduction and integration of technology, physically and symbolically, into everyday routines' (Stenning et al 2010: 73). To date, very little social science literature has used domestication to conceptualize household food practices. But domestication offers a useful framework for analysing how the marketplace is mediated in the domestic consumption of food. That is, it allows us to factor in how conflicting marketized tensions (around authenticity, for example) impact on domestic meal provisioning. As a concept, it sheds light on the processes by which food comes to represent the values of the home: 'the process of consumption and of embedding the object into the household is one of sense making, of transforming the alien object to ascribe it with meaning in the symbolic reality of the household' (Berker et al 2006: 7).

Silverstone and Haddon (1996) note that consumer commitment to and negotiation of processes of domestication act as a signifier of their participation in consumption. Particular forms of domestication then reflect and reproduce household capital. This is because consumers are negotiating classed frameworks which both facilitate access to and position particular goods as worthy of domestication. This can be extended to the provision of food. Paying attention to the discerning processes through which food comes to be selected from the marketplace and transformed into a substance for feeding demarcates a process through which household identities are formed. Insofar as domestication involves resistance (to microwave meals for example) *and* accommodation (of culturally valued foods from culturally valued places) it is clearly related to class as I will demonstrate in later chapters. This is reflected in debate about cookbooks for instance. Cookbooks are material and cultural artefacts, which, employed in the domestic kitchen, can act as manuals for the domestication of food. Several studies highlight the changing focus of contemporary cookbooks, which reflect and reproduce social frameworks (Brownlie, Hewer and Horne 2005; Gallegos 2005; Cappellini and Parsons 2014; Hewer 2016). Cappellini and Parsons (2014) for example, note that the role of cookbooks extends far beyond the preparation of food in the domestic sphere to include advice on selecting the 'right' ingredients from the 'right' places. This means that cultural capital can be displayed through consumption: shopping skill and selecting the right products. Moreover, as I hope to show, paying attention to the types of cookbooks which individuals use in the process of transforming ingredients into meals can highlight the public narratives with which participants identify and the types of practices they deem worthy of investment. That said, domestication is a complex process which extends beyond class display. It is a process that is related to the material and social contexts of household lives. Given this observation, let us turn to literature about time to provide a starting point for analysing how objects deemed to have little value come to be domesticated in contested ways. Paying attention to the temporalities of domestic consumption adds another, important, layer to the analysis that follows because it accounts for the material and social constraints under which domestication occurs.

Time

Food and time are inevitably connected: it takes time to source, prepare and eat food, and food and eating are also ways of marking and organizing time. Meals are sequentially connected and exist in relation to each other (Douglas 1975): lunch follows breakfast for example. There is a range of sociological research about the ramifications of time in the domestic sphere. Some of this takes food as its empirical focus, and much of it centres on gender. Establishing a framework for understanding the relationship between the multiple temporal elements of food consumption in the home, requires a critical overview of these different approaches. Studies which have quantitatively analysed patterns of domestic time-use have been useful for highlighting the gendered division of domestic labour, and when and how practices vary (Sullivan 1997; Mancino and Newman 2006; Warde et al 2007). For instance, Sullivan's (1997) research into the gendered experience of domestic time found that while cooking fell high on the list of domestic activities performed by men, this was generally done alongside their partner. The women on the other hand mainly cooked alone, suggesting that there is an element of 'gendered supervision' in domestic cooking. Studies such as these are useful in explaining generic time usage; they do, however, fall short of probing the deeper meanings attributed to the activities they are intended to measure. Moreover, time is not linear, and therefore not breakdown-able into measurable, quantifiable units. Analysing time as a unit of measurement fails to grasp the ways in which social practices are related to time, and how different time constraints organize and construct the experiences of activities (Southerton 2006).

If we understand social action as practices, we can see that their temporality is better understood in terms of fluid and intersecting rhythms, sequences and periodicities rather than strictly defined tasks with objectively measurable timings. In other words, practices involve interwoven 'timespaces' (Schatzki 2009: 40). As well as being founded on body habits and learnt taste, the practice of eating and cooking, an everyday and routine activity, is connected temporally and spatially to other practices. Time constraints both organize the rhythms of domestic food practices and impact on how practices are experienced. For instance, as Blake et al (2009) find, the practice of bulk cooking during the weekend may be undertaken to free up timespaces during the working week. The family meal provides a useful means of illustrating the importance of adopting a multidimensional approach to time for the analysis of domestic food practices. This is because an added complexity for family meals is that in addition to planning and provisioning, they require that members of the household are together at a particular time in a particular place to eat. For instance, Brannen, et al (2013; see also O'Connell and Brannen 2016) draw on the concept of synchronicity to analyse how dual earner households coordinate often conflicting 'time-space paths' of household members to facilitate family meals.

Family is not a 'single, homogeneous and timeless entity' (Jackson 2009: 4) to which individuals belong, but rather a fluid and dynamic process which is (re)made and (re)done through practices (Curtis et al 2009, Green et al 2009; James and Curtis 2010). Just as domestic food practices communicate our identity (what we are and what we are not), they are also a way to 'do' family. Several studies have identified the family meal as integral to the doing of family (Charles and Kerr 1988; Devault 1991; Bugge and Almås 2006; Cappellini and Parsons 2012). At the same time, media, political and even academic narratives indicate that the family meal is waning. Research by Daniels et al (2012), for example, starts from the hypothesis that the family meal is in decline and that this is cause for concern. And yet there is a lack of evidence that the family meal is in decline (Murcott 1997, 2012; Warde and Martens 2000; Jackson et al 2009; Wilk 2010), or at risk of 'extinction' (Cappellini et al 2016a: 247). Marshall, Cappellini and Parsons (2016) argue that the family dinner is one of the most enduring modes of eating meals. Similarly, Warde and Yates (2017) found that in Britain, of people living in shared households, 90 per cent of their evening meals were shared with others. Nor is there evidence that if such a trend were underway that this is cause for concern. Nevertheless, the family meal remains discursively reproduced as an idealized practice. Southerton (2003) argues that the socio-temporal organization of daily practices has changed because of deroutinization and informalization. In other words, the fragmentation of collectively organized temporality means that the scheduling of domestic collective practices, such as the family meal, has become an individual's responsibility rather than a matter of wider communal traditions and conventions (dinner at 6 pm after the male breadwinner's workday has finished, for example). It follows then, that household prioritization of the family meal, despite changes which make eating together hard to achieve, is evidence of its ideological durability. For instance, while participants in Backett-Milburn et al's study (2010) only ate together half of the time, they all indicated a preference for family meals. Importantly, the justifications around not eating as a family centred on other conflicting practices, such as work and sport. The shortcomings of not staging the family meal were offset by the appropriate balance of other activities that were also a highly valorized site of doing 'good' family and class.

Prioritizing certain activities (such as sharing food or cooking from scratch) highlights two things: that some activities have more cultural value than others and that some individuals have an increased capacity to negotiate time constraints. Looking first at capacity to negotiate time constraints, Southerton (2006) found that participants with high education levels were more likely to create diverse temporal spaces to synchronize and coordinate a variety of practices than participants with lower education levels. Clearly there is a correlation of temporal autonomy with dominant capital, but this also highlights that there is cultural value associated with diverse cultural participation. Given that, as I have argued previously, the handling of diverse cultural forms acts as a marker of distinction, then it seems fair to suggest that handling diverse time-space paths also acts as a marker of distinction. Second, paying attention to which practices are prioritized amid conflicting and diverse temporal spaces indicates which practices are valued. Understanding how participants dedicate time to food, then, is an important means of understanding the cultural value of eating and feeding in particular ways.

The consumption of convenience foods provides an interesting object of analysis to expand on the relationship between time constraints and the values attached to foods and ways of eating. As Jackson and Viehoff (2016) point out, definitions of 'convenience' are wide-ranging: from fast foods, to mass-produced foods, to foods which are easily prepared. For instance, bagged lettuce, filleted fish and frozen ready meals all count as convenience foods (Meah and Jackson 2017). What these foods share is that they provide a solution to problems of timing by enabling 'the relaxation of constraints on the individual's trajectory through time and space' (Warde 1999: 522). They allow food provisioning to be broken down into different processes and reassembled to fit complex and sometimes hurried temporal routines. At the same time however, 'convenience' has negative moral connotations and is frequently associated with laziness and unhealthiness (Parsons 2016). This is related to the opposition between convenience and care identified by Warde (1997), which I suggest is both classed and gendered. For instance, while feeding the family with a ready meal may be an efficient use of time, a reliance on convenience can involve compromising norms of care around the provision of food cooked from scratch. Nonetheless, Warde's antonym of convenience and care can arguably also be reconciled and the relationship between the poles is fluid and contextual. Meah and Jackson's (2017) research shows how participants drew on multiple notions of care in relation to their provision of convenience foods to the household. These ranged from caring about reducing the waste attached to homemade, to using convenience as a strategy to devote more time to care for family members.

Who's cooking? Gender and doing family through food

The extent to which practices such as sharing food or cooking are coordinated or prioritized is associated with cultural and social orientations towards eating in particular ways. Furthermore, the requirement to organize practices into particular slots of time as well as the responsibility of synchronizing household members to share food, for example, depends on household members' relationships to the constraints of time. Time constraints shape how practices are experienced, but the ability to negotiate the temporal constraints of practices also relates to an individual's position within social relations. Different groups experience feeling 'harried' (Southerton 2003) in relation to different practices and their associated norms. This point allows me to factor gender as well as class into the analysis. There is a wealth of literature which establishes that, despite their increased participation in the workforce, women remain responsible for feeding the household (Beagan et al 2008, 2015; O'Connell and Brannen 2016; Parsons 2016; Yates and Warde 2017), and the coordination of the family meal by mothers has long historical roots (Davis et al 2016). If family identities are actively established, reinforced, and organized by patterns of practices, then the prevailing responsibility of women to coordinate everyday food provisioning highlights their centrality in the production of family. These practices reflect hegemonic discourses about family, which combined, impact on how people organize family lives. For example, by paying attention to the invisible nature of foodwork (such as planning), DeVault's (1991) research reminds us that domestic feeding is socially organized and naturalized as feminine. DeVault also shows that through their responsibility for feeding the family, the women in her study were maintaining and producing the family according to classed and gendered frameworks.

Yates and Warde (2017) found that men are more likely to have their household meals prepared for them than their female counterparts. It seems reasonable to argue therefore that being responsible for feeding work, women are disproportionately affected by time constraints. At the same time, there has been a renewed emphasis on homemade food in recent years, which is often positioned against the increased availability of convenience foods. Returning to Warde's (1997) antonym of convenience and care for a moment, public narratives circulate which demonize convenience because it undermines spending time on preparing 'good', healthy meals from scratch. Accounting for the temporality of practices highlights how classed femininity operates via feeding since the subversion of care for convenience in the face of temporal constraints is understood to contravene acceptable standards of (classed) femininity. The working women in Thompson's (1996) study talked of striking a compromise within this antonym by using pressure cookers, slow cookers, and microwaves. These 'time-shifting devices' (Warde 1999: 522) enabled the scheduling of feeding within fragmented slots of time. Moreover, like some women in Moisio et al's (2004) study, the women also relied on convenience foods to feed their family to gain time and efficiency. However, given that care through feeding is discursively constructed as feminine, it is unsurprising that using convenience foods was a source of guilt for many of these women. Convenience food is 'tinged with moral disapprobation' (Warde 1999: 518) after all. Homemade food, by contrast, is positioned as individual and distant from homogenized, mass-produced food, and its symbolic value is intimately tied to gendered caregiving and domesticity. The provision of homemade food requires an active commitment to a particular mode of feeding as having value. To this end, convenience food is domesticated in contested ways because it requires few active practices of conversion.

The scant body of literature which focuses on men's experience of cooking (Szabo 2012, 2014; Klasson and Ulver 2015; Neuman et al 2017) establishes the nuanced ways that masculine identities are configured through cooking, and how these depart from the feminized forms I discussed earlier. Men are increasingly participating in domestic cooking, especially when their female partners work full time (O'Connell and Brannen 2016). Significantly, research establishes that women remain responsible for the cooking with men often adopting a supportive role or enacting 'special-occasion' cooking (O'Connell and Brannen 2016). Klasson and Ulver (2015) argue the male participants in their study dramatized mundane domestic food practices so as to conduct a performance of hegemonic masculinity. Nevertheless, while women's cooking is seen as 'other-oriented responsibility' and men's as 'self-orientated leisure' (Szabo 2014: 18), Szabo's male participants who had significant domestic feeding responsibilities presented a more nuanced picture. Szabo argues that many of the men in his study drew on traditional 'feminine' care-orientated approaches to food, suggesting that the self/other dichotomy can be contested. This is an important insight; however, it remains within a framework which conceptualizes care-oriented foodwork as feminine and does not dismantle that.

It is clear that the provision of food acts as to produce a socially and culturally acceptable feminine identity (Bugge and Almås 2006; Haukanes 2007; Parsons 2014; Harman and Cappellini 2015). This is not to suggest that norms around feeding are passively reproduced, rather to highlight that they are ever-present. Indeed, women in Beagan et al's (2008) study discussed their feeding work, not in terms of gendered responsibility, but in terms of individual decisions, employing rationales such as wanting to feed the family healthy, high-quality foods. Likewise, Bugge and Almås (2006) show how cooking dinner is not just an act of caring for the family as noted by Charles and Kerr (1988), but it also operates as a kind of identity work to position the female self via socially and culturally valid food practices. While Bugge and Almås' (2006) research falls short in explaining how valued food practices relate to class, a number of studies specifically attend to gender and class (Parsons 2014, Beagan 2015; Ehlert 2021). What is notable about these studies is the way that food practices demarcate classed and gendered boundaries. For instance, middle-class mothers in Parson's (2014) study demonstrated a commitment to homemade to differentiate themselves from the cultural symbol of a working-class mother who feeds her family convenience foods. It is important then to situate such commitments within a complex web of spatiotemporal constraints and pressures within which the domestic provisioning of food is situated.

Conclusion

Food is experienced and accessed differently along classed and gendered lines, meaning that food practices and 'choices' must be understood in relation to the cultural and social spaces within which people consume. I started this chapter by arguing for the salient existence of class, but I noted that as a concept it needs to be mobilized in relation to individualism. In this framing, it becomes possible to investigate how food practices and perspectives link with classed identities which are lived in relation to other social divisions. By building on Bourdieu's concepts of habitus, capital, field, and practice I take the lived experience of food in the home as my point of analysis. Through the concept of habitus, I argue that the middle classes have the capital to reproduce and engage with the hierarchies of value relating to good food. I have argued that despite the field of consumption being fragmented, hierarchies of taste and distinction continue to validate individual choices. By focusing on the materialities of food, I have established how everyday practices are interrelated and organized in socio-temporal contexts. In addition, I have worked with the concept of domestication to encapsulate the active process by which food is selected externally and embedded with symbolic value to make it fit for purpose. This is particularly pertinent when considered in relation to my earlier arguments which are that identities are valued in relation to reflexive and individualized involvement in the consumption process. These ways of conceptualizing everyday practices are a way of gaining a more nuanced understanding of how good taste is reproduced, even when taste preferences are said to be increasingly fragmented. Chapters 3, 4 and 5 will draw on these conceptual foundations, and in so doing will challenge the rhetoric that 'good' foods can be accessed through the simple provision of knowledge and finance.

3

Talking Food: Classed Narratives, Social Identities and Biographical Transitions

This chapter speaks to debates around notions of individualism, reflexivity and choice. It has two main foci. First, I show how the centrality of individuality in participant narratives reproduces (classed) ideas that individual and reflexive food consumption is central to the makings of identity. A theme of *not* belonging to collective categories such as class, emerges across the sample, but the repeated pattern of distancing from group belongingness I see as indicative of some form of collective recognition which operates around the notion of being individual. From this, I suggest that participants' propensity to narrate a position of individuality can be situated within a broader discursive framework of consumerism within which notions of individual choice dominate. Second, I place theoretical emphasis on practices and dispositions as a manifestation of a continual 'point of suture' (Hall 1996: 6) between the self and (classed) social position. I consider participant biographical data through a socio-historical lens, noting that going to university, travelling and establishing households emerged as key moments in coming-of-age food stories. Drawing on participant narratives of mobility, I note that personal transition points involving the acquisition of capital often go hand-in-hand with encountering, and honing, understandings of 'good' taste. Regardless of chronological age, what emerges from these stories is that the expansion of tastes is understood as a consequence of globalization and relatedly, the increase of diversity, abundance and choice in the field of food consumption. Considering participants' experience of taste expansion in a broader social context, I question the extent to which a consumerist ideology, which stipulates the centrality of individual choice, impacts on their orientations towards consuming diversity.

Unique identities

Before exploring how food features in life histories, I want to first unpick how participants 'see' themselves as classed (or not). I have noted previously that class is a contentious concept. This is not limited to the conceptual realms of sociological debate. Participant narratives about class highlight the conceptual slippiness and fuzziness of class, despite it being employed (or variations of the term) in everyday contexts as what follows will show. I asked about class at the end of the first interview and many participants offered lengthy responses. As Steve's reply shows, these narratives provide a rich starting point from which to consider the complex and often conflicting ways that participants reflected about themselves as classed. He elaborated on a recent conversation he had had with his partner:

KG:	So would you identify as belonging to a particular social class?
Steve (35–44):	It's a funny question this because, you know, bizarrely we all ... I had this discussion with [partner] because we both come from very much working-class families, my family tradition comes from pit-yackers,[1] you know from the pits as well. And [partner]'s family's very much, not necessarily from the pits, but they're very much working class. But if you look at ... you look at you know our salaries, where we live, how we socialize as well, we are very much middle class now which is a bit ... bit of a surprise for us really because we kind of ... kind of ... kind of think we're probably working class but we are probably very much stuck in that middle class I suppose as well.
KG:	Hmm-mm. What about when you were growing up? Did you feel working class then or ...?
Steve:	I think because my parents were the first generation for around about six or seven years who weren't in the mines, weren't from the mining stock ... they moved away from the traditional pit villages where all my grandparents lived until they died. And they were the first generation who actually went into a career away from that. So my dad ran his own business from the age of 25 and while my mother took time out to look after us when she was young,

---

[1] Pit-yacker is a Northern English colloquial term for coal miner.

she was very highly skilled at the job she did at the [name of organization]. So if you spoke to them they would probably say they were middle class as well. But I still felt very working class because the rest of the extended family hadn't moved away from the pit villages.

Steve's expression of classed identity highlights the complex and often conflicting ways in which class exists in both social structures ('our salaries, where we live, how we socialize as well, we are very much middle class now') and individual selves and emotional registers ('I still felt very working class'). His ambivalence and uncertainty about characterizing himself as middle class is indicated in his response that he and is partner 'are probably very much *stuck* in that middle class I *suppose*' which is a 'bit of a surprise'. Steve clearly gives precedence to the durability of his working-class habitus, indicating the strength of gravity of class in his biography: he feels working class on account of his family heritage in mining. This is despite his parents never having been directly involved in the pit. By his own recognition, Steve can be positioned as middle class on account of his capital, his parents would claim a middle-class identity, and Steve has not experienced downward mobility. Nevertheless, Steve is reluctant to let go of his working-class heritage because of his extended family's attachments to the pit community.

Almost half of the sample drew on aspects of working-classness in relation to their own personal biography and like Steve, this often entailed eliciting a binary opposition of working class and middle class. My point here is not to dispute the diverse ways in which class mobility is experienced, but to draw attention to the limiting effects of conceptualizing personal mobility by setting out working class and middle class as mutually exclusive. As the separate excerpts that follow suggest, it positions a middle-class identity as either something that can be either had or not, leaving little space for anything in between:

Julie (35–44):   And you know we're both, is it white collar workers still? You know we're both professional so ... I dunno, I'm not sure I do fulfil the middle-class bracket or are we still working class? I'm not sure. I wouldn't know, cause I'm definitely ... we're both definitely working class. Well my dad with him being a policeman was a professional, you know, I don't know.

Sara (25–34):   I wouldn't say that I'm working class because ... I guess it comes ... you know kind of ... it probably does come down to money, like I earn a good salary. So I would say that if I was to class myself as working

> class, in the traditional sense, I guess maybe I wouldn't have gone to university. I wouldn't be on the salary that I'm on. But I don't … I absolutely don't see myself as middle class, at all. I mean I've got friends who perhaps might fit into that kind of box and I feel like they're different to me. So I … I feel like I'm in this weird space between … I dunno, it's a bit strange.

Again, there is a sense of ambiguity and insecurity in these narratives about class identity. For Julie and Sara, it seems that asserting a middle-class identity, entails leaving behind working-class aspects of their habitus, leaving them uncertain: 'I don't know' they both say at the end of their response. These responses suggest that it is difficult to narrate a classed sense of self via personal history when we are limited to speaking about class as a binary of being either working class or middle class. Resultantly, as Sara suggests, when participants find themselves in this 'weird space between', their sense of class belonging becomes less easy to articulate. Nonetheless, these participants appear certain about not being middle class: 'I absolutely don't see myself as middle class, at all' (Sara); 'we're both definitely working class' (Julie).

Many participants appeared driven to anchor themselves as distant from being middle class. Friedman, O'Brien and McDonald (2021) ask why professional people (mis)identify as working class, finding that even participants from privileged upbringings forged affinities to working-class extended family histories. Similarly in this study, my participants drew on experiences, some of which were related to their parents' (or even, as we see with Steve, grandparents') upbringings, to find a link, however tenuous, to working-classness. From being brought up in a single parent family, living on a council estate, through to parents owning their own business, a myriad of experiences and contexts was shoehorned into the category of working class. In these framings, working class appears to be shorthand for anything which lies outside of the narrow parameters of participant perceptions of middle class. The irony, however, is that in marking themselves as distant from being middle class, these narratives reproduce a hierarchical polarization of a classed dualism. Despite being rich in economic and educational capital, Julie notes that she is unsure that she and her husband '*fulfil* the middle-class bracket', suggesting that she is unsure whether she meets the requirements for claiming a middle-class identity. Yet conceptualizing middle-classness as something to be achieved positions a middle-class identity as exclusive effectively positioning that which is not middle class as a negative other.

Participant accounts which emphasized working-class aspects of their biography also offer insight into how forms of distinction can operate around disidentifying with the privileges associated with being middle class. As the excerpts suggest, *being* middle class could be understood as a limiting category from which many participants actively and ostensibly distanced themselves. It is well documented that for those who are low on capital, to be working class carries little more than social stigmatization (Skeggs 1997; Lawler 1999; Reay 2005; Tyler 2008, 2015; Reay, Crozier and James 2011). However, being positioned on the higher rungs of the class ladder, one can both legitimize identity categories which are not open to all as positive and resist a middle-class identity because to be middle class is to acknowledge that one is a product of social positions rich in capital. This in turn echoes a public narrative of meritocracy which reproduces the idea that working hard and taking advantage of opportunities leads to success as opposed to privilege or luck. To use the words of Friedman, O'Brien and McDonald, while this 'intergenerational self' reflects the lived experience of multigenerational upward mobility, it also obscures class privilege. It 'simultaneously casts their own achievements as unusually meritocratically legitimate while erasing the structural privileges that have shaped key moments in their trajectories' (2021: 717).

Granted, questions about class can 'tap … a nerve' (Savage et al 2015: 5) but it is not that my participants appeared to distance themselves from class as such, but from belonging to the category of being middle class in a straightforward way. Participants appeared to recognize the existence of class, yet the ambiguous and often lengthy nature of their accounts of class belonging suggests that thinking about class in relation to themselves is a complex process. Supporting arguments that class identities are expressed through marking boundaries of self and other, their narratives of class belonging also contained many relational references. Thomas' account demonstrates this powerfully:

'We sometimes do buy the Telegraph on a weekend, or if we can't get the Observer, you know and they talk about the middle class and they always talk about the middle class going on skiing holidays and children at private school and all this kind of stuff. Well, we don't do that stuff. My children didn't go to private school, you know they went to the local comprehensive. So we you know … I don't quite know how one defines these things and … but from the Telegraph's point of view we're definitely not middle class. We've lived professional lives, we've been educated, we've got degrees and whatever else and had professional lives and things, so we sort of think, well we can't be … we don't think we're working class (laughs) … probably somewhere in the middle, lower middle (laughs).' (Thomas, 65+)

Similarly to Steve, Julie and Sara's accounts, Thomas appears reluctant to offer a simple class identity. His explanation draws on relational identifications to others from which he distinguishes himself, a mediatized picture of middle-class practices of private education and ski holidays, for example. Skeggs (2005) notes that distance from middle-class identities can act as means of avoiding the discursive positioning of the middle classes as pretentious. But at the same time, Thomas jokes: 'well we can't be ... we don't think we're working class'. He eventually arrives at a class position which is 'somewhere in the middle, lower middle' (as opposed to upper working). What is particularly important here is that as later analysis will demonstrate, while many participants positioned themselves away from being plainly middle class, they embodied and valued cultural characteristics which are discursively positioned as middle class. This is especially so when we pay attention to everyday food practices; classed categories emerged via the construction of a negatively imagined working-class other.

While many respondents located themselves within a binary of middle and working class, some participants drew on other categories to offer a reflexive account of classed identity which implicitly worked to disrupt their classed positionality. Des' account illustrates this further:

'Well clearly middle class and I know all about the ... you know I'm what's it? A? Cause the professional, social ... the different ... so I know I'm in that professional ... I also know that class is fluid so I know there's sort of the ... you know I'm in the lucky position of being quite well off. The sort of Jewish aspect is ... that does muddy the water cause I know that sort of ... the construction of things like you know ethnicity and ... it's so odd that you know how people ... how people are seen as Jewish. So our kids, because [wife] isn't Jewish, are not Jewish (laughs) according to the Müllers, but they see ... they will see themselves as having a Jewish identity cause of having the thing of Seder nights and ... Seder nights, bagels and hummus. So I think ... see a mix of things ... so would think probably middle class, professional, ethnicity is sort of white ... see I always don't know ... white British Jewish, I never know quite what to add in so I always write sort of I'd prefer not to.' (Des, 55–64)

Des offers a somewhat sociological perspective about class, noting his awareness of its fluidity and its intersection with other categories, such as ethnicity, which 'muddy the water'. He moves from being 'clearly middle class' to thinking he is '*probably* middle class' which at first glance suggests that he is 'putting together, dismantling and rearranging' his identity (Bauman 2009: 10). To some extent, reflexive distancing from collective groupings echoes the claims of postmodernism that as individualization flourishes, established group categories, such as class, are no longer anchored to identities. For instance, Beck argued that 'processes of individualization *deprive class distinctions of their social identity*' (1992: 100; italics original). As Des' narrative illustrates, identities are fragmented and fractured. But as I will go on to argue, the ways in which participants worked to displace class from themselves, is in fact indicative of wider class processes.

Des uses the example of food to illustrate the intersectionality of his identity. Food is widely understood to be significant in reinforcing ethnic belongingness because it represents an everyday materialization of ethnic identity (Cappellini and Yen 2013). While Des no longer keeps a kosher diet, he retains aspects of Jewish eating traditions and practices such as Seder night. Similarly to Steve's reference to his family's connections to the pit, these food traditions appear to be an important means of maintaining a Jewish identity across the generations and clearly take precedence over reflecting on his classed sense of self. At other points in our interviews however, Des explicitly marked some of the food he eats as classed. The following exchange occurred while he described the contents of the fridge:

Des: This is wild garlic pesto. I mean how middle class can you get (laughs)?
KG: (laughs) Can I take a photo of it? (Figure 3.1)
Des: So I got that from that place in the Grainger Market.
KG: Oh [name of deli]?
Des: Yes, so I said 'Give me your most middle-class condiment' (laughs).

This exchange reinforces the relationality of class between Des and I, since I, like him, understand that you can buy 'middle-class' condiments in the Grainger Market and that wild garlic pesto 'counts' as hyper middle class in the first place. Contrary to Des' rather unstable account of class identity, where he notes he is 'probably middle class', in this exchange he is clear in coding some foods as middle class. Importantly, these classed markers are positioned as external to himself. This account is framed with laughter suggesting a mutual knowingness of the classed credentials attached to the pesto. Humour can be used to bypass awkward juxtapositions in everyday food encounters (Jackson and Meah 2019), working as a form of 'ironic distancing' (Lawler 2005: 437). While this draws attention to the symbolic capital attached to certain foods, it also highlights the complex dynamics of Des' self-knowledge. Des indicates that eating a wild garlic variation of pesto bought from a delicatessen is a middle-class practice. He appears aware that he is enacting a type of identity which could be conceived as pretentious, drawing attention to his awareness through humour. The level of reflexivity he demonstrates about the classed aspects of the pesto almost situates middle-classness as a subjective performance which can be invested in during particular moments.

Figure 3.1: Researcher photo of Des' wild garlic pesto

Boyne notes that expressions of class are marked by reflexive self-awareness (such as being 'rueful, ironic, envious, reflectively proud') in postmodern times (2002: 119). To this I would add that in an individualistic culture, there is *value* in actively finding multiple ways of maintaining one's sense of self as unique. Moreover, the ability to enact valued ways of being with recourse to reflexivity is an indicator of the resources one has to hand. Echoing Skeggs, 'the imperative towards extraordinary public subjectivity' is central to the 'making of the exchange-value middle-class self', and it is through these processes that class relations are made (2005: 974). While it is through distance from, or multi-membership of, social groupings that participants carved a self which is unique, collective social groupings such as class were ever-present in their narratives. Contrary to Beck's argument, this sample exhibited shared traits and practices suggesting that class operates around individual displays associated with desirable (middle-class) 'modes of individualization' (Savage 2000). Moreover, while participants demonstrated a reluctance to articulate a sense of belonging to being middle class (often identifying with a working class 'intergenerational self' instead (Friedman et al 2021), at the same time an imagined working-class other often emerged in participant accounts about practices as a reference point from which to evaluate themselves and others, as I will now explore.

Relations of otherness

While subjective accounts of class identity were often ambiguous and fragmented, as is suggested from my exchange with Des, food that carries symbolic capital was generally aligned with the middle classes. I want to now turn to data which suggest that markings of distinctions in relation to food and feeding operate in relation to a classed other. The processes and forms this distinction takes will be looked at in further detail in the next chapter. The three separate examples that follow, which are drawn from participants who identified with middle-class upbringings, expand on this further. They are responses to my asking the participants to reflect on the extent to which class has impacted on their relationship to food. I begin with a quote from Neil; he invokes class by referring to both his professional and personal qualities to talk about health and obesity.

Neil (45–54):	I mentioned Rotherham. So I did a project down in Rotherham and we worked for [organization] and that's the most unrelentingly working-class area that I have ever been to and I mean Jamie Oliver did a food programme. It, yeah ... and seeing ... seeing fat people in wheelchairs ... I'm quite fattist; that is a prejudice you know so seeing grossly obese people sitting in wheelchairs with a fag in one hand and a bag of chips on their lap, wheeling themselves round the town. And seeing massive queues outside the chip shop every lunch time.
Juliette (35–44):	Sometimes I look at my shopping trolley and I look at somebody else's shopping trolley and you know they'll have lots of ... I don't know, crispy pancakes and pop and stuff like that and then their trolley looks very different from mine, because I'll have you know, lettuce and ... fresh fish or whatever and yes ... and I'm very aware that it's a difference in budget really.

Carla (45–54):   Yeah, I think they are really. Sadly … and that's obviously pretty clear up here [in the North East] still I think. It is an issue. I feel like it's an issue at school. I look at … I kind of … why do you have sweets every day after school? Why would you give your kids sweets *every day* after school? I don't understand it. It's so obvious and you watch them. I've watched these kids, they look a little bit tubby in year two and you get to year 6 and this girl is like this (motions fatness with arms). It's like, what planet are you on, parent? I don't understand it. I feel like schools should be actively engaged with that. It's a responsibility thing. I mean that poor girl, you know, it's tough.

KG: Do you think that's to do with class?

Carla: (pause) I don't know. I wouldn't say that's the only factor. It's unlikely to be the only factor. And you know, is it class? Is it just … some of its regional heritage, I think …

KG: Yeah. Ok and then do you think that belonging to a particular class has influenced your own food tastes?

Carla: Tastes. I dunno …

KG: Or your practices?

Carla: Well yeah. I think it's just inevitable, you're around other people who are all doing it. You know, we all care about food, we all like to prepare fresh food, we talk about food, definitely.

Relational othering and marking boundaries are fundamental to the construction of the middle-class identity (Bourdieu 1984). These accounts vary in explicitness, but the point I want to make here is that these accounts not only implicitly project negative value onto a working-class other but also clearly code the working classes as knowable. I had asked the participants to reflect about how class impacted on *their* relationship to food, but rather than generate data about the extent to which participants felt classed, class is talked about through the construction a negative classed other. Although somewhat hyperbolic, Neil's depiction of 'grossly obese people sitting in wheelchairs with a fag in one hand and a bag of chips on their lap' is a function of their being the product of an 'unrelentingly working-class area'. Interestingly, he is reflexive about his prejudice towards fatness, but not about his class racism, despite openly marking the working classes 'as a race apart' (Gidley and Rooke 2010: 112). While not explicit, Carla and Juliette implicitly construct a classed other. In the lengthy excerpt from Carla, she moves from answering a question about class belongingness with an example of other parents feeding children sweets, towards the ensuing uncertainty and hesitancy she articulates when asked if her example is to do with class and how class has affected her food tastes and practices. Likewise, Juliette juxtaposes crispy pancakes and pop with fresh fish and lettuce but appears reluctant to use the term class when she concludes her response with 'and I'm very aware that it's ... it's a difference in budget really.' While Juliette and Carla appear hesitant to name class, their accounts nonetheless situate their classed existence as relational by projecting class onto a negative other. Considered in relation to arguments which suggest that this is *necessary* in order to situate the self as being the site of proper, desirable and responsible personhood (Lawler 2005; Skeggs 2005), these accounts do construct a working class which is knowable on account of not being like 'us'. Clearly from the complex biographical narratives outlined these participants do not represent a homogenous middle class. Nevertheless, there appeared to be a recurrent pattern across the sample that thinking about class entails the construction of a relational group of people, who are marked as undesirable. Articulated through distance and individualization, participants voiced a shared understanding about taste, indicating a form of class allegiance and belonging. As Carla suggests, 'we [the middle classes] all care about food, we all like to prepare fresh food, we talk about food'.

The second point I would like to make is that not only is there an assumption that a working-class other can be coded, but it is coded as negative for the consumption of the wrong sorts of foods. Accounts about food and class implicitly constructed an imagined other whose consumption choices are irresponsible, vulgar, excessive and without taste. Again, the separate excerpts that follow are in response to my asking about the influence of class on *their* food tastes and preferences:

KG:	What about food choices, or food, in your life, has that ever made you feel aware of class?
Fiona (65+):	Yeah, sure. When you see people giving their toddlers Gregg's sausage rolls to eat in the pram followed by a can of Coke you think, don't do it (laughs)!
Linda (45–54):	I think we're all quite snobbish in a way. I mean I think I'd walk past a pizza place or a takeaway and go 'oh that looks like a dive' or a greasy spoon, you know all-day breakfast-type place and think 'oh I'm not going in there' (laughs), which can be unfair I know.
Harriet (55–64):	Well yes again because food is classist isn't it? Because you tend to sort of look down on the people who just eat McDonalds or processed food or whatever.

Food has long since been a marker for class in Great Britain (James 1997; Warde 1997). Hence, evidence of participants erecting classed boundaries around certain foods is unsurprising. It is nevertheless important to spend some time unpacking how this played out in participants' narratives, since narratives of not being like 'them' seemed to underpin so much of what participants said and did. This will be looked at in more detail in the following chapter, which specifically focuses on the complexities of everyday food practices. But the point I want to make here is that Fiona's laughter, Linda's acknowledgement that her assumption 'can be unfair' and Harriet's rhetorical question that 'food is classist isn't it?' all demonstrate an awareness of a 'classing gaze' (Gidley and Rooke 2010: 95). This gaze which these participants ostensibly observe and perform aligns devalued foods and ways of eating with an imagined classed other. The foods named are cheap, but it is not as Juliette suggested previously that 'it's a difference in budget'. These participants appear to produce relational judgements about *their* classed sense of self by drawing on cultural and moral aspects of consumption which function to produce a classed other who is feckless (giving children in pushchairs Coke and Gregg's pasties, or sweets every day after school), eats in dirty establishments ('it looks like a dive'), excessive and vulgar (grossly obese people with chips on their knee and a fag in their hand) and limited to *only* eating the wrong sorts of food ('who just eat McDonalds or processed food'). In what follows, I consider how the taste hierarchy is maintained in the dialectical relationship between classed social positioning and food dispositions.

Hierarchies of taste

In Britain, in the late 19th century class status and distinction were dependent on the adoption of French cuisine (James 1997). Today, although the available ingredients and culinary reference points have changed, culinary taste plays a significant role in the formation of the middle-class identity. In particular, notions of authenticity are attached to claims of distinction, meaning that an array of foods can carry cultural value, so long as they can be verified according to frames of heritage, locality and personal connection for example. The exchange here, between Carla and I, illustrates this dynamic further:

Carla: You can have your earthy Spanish big stew with a hunk of bread, that still looks nice, but you can also have a very, you know bit of food on the plate that's very careful and …
KG: And for you is there a …?
Carla: Oh well I think I like them all.
KG: Do you?

Carla: Yeah. But, you know, I don't really want to see like a big pasty on … you know that's really greasy with nothing green on it. But you know, if it's a really good Cornish pasty that's really freshly … then that's going to be great. So, I think you can have … in music I would say, for me there's kind of good quality, well you could call it good quality light music, or you know, sort of, fizzy music … you know, it's kind of … it's not deep but it's still … it's well crafted. So you can have the same … you know, I love a good fry up, but it needs to be a good fry up. I don't want it to be like you know, all the egg to be dried and the sausages to be full of fat, you know. You want to have, you know, the nice fried tomatoes and your mushrooms that are really done well, and your really good black pudding, but I'm still going to enjoy a really good fry up. So you can have good quality bad food in inverted commas. But you couldn't eat that … even that good quality fry up, you couldn't eat that every day, because that's obviously going to be really unhealthy. But it's nice to enjoy it once in a while.

This account reveals two things. First, by drawing on frames of authenticity and tradition, certain foods can be positioned as having value. Carla is specific that the pasty is Cornish and that the earthy stew is Spanish. This highlights that distinction is not about rejecting traditional British food in favour of 'classy', French food as it once was but is rather attached to the correct appraisal of authenticity. Second, Carla negotiates a tension between 'democracy and distinction' (Johnston and Baumann 2014), suggesting that the taste hierarchy can be broken down and that different cultural forms can be appreciated equally. On one hand, Carla's account appears to be inclusive in positioning a fry up alongside the 'earthy Spanish stew' or food which has been carefully arranged on a plate, implying that different types of food are equal and can be offered as vehicles of good taste. On the other hand, the taste hierarchy remains intact through the fine distinctions that the pasty is fresh, or that the individual components of the fry up need to be done well to be appreciated. Carla also evokes an interesting comparison between food and another form of culture: with 'good quality light music' which is 'not deep' but 'well crafted', indicating how classed positioning around food occurs in relation to other forms of cultural capital. Her comparison also highlights how popular cultural forms (those which are 'not deep') can be positioned as having value by attaching ideas of skill to the processes of their production (those which are 'well-crafted'). At the same time, it is through recognizing this simplicity that complexity can be attached to the process of appreciation. In this way, her narrative can be read as a demonstration of the ways in which a capacity to decode the apparent ordinariness of certain foods can act to showcase an ability to legitimize even 'bad food'. Finally, Carla positions herself as distinguishable from someone who might eat a fry up every day, by concluding that even though she enjoys 'good quality bad food', she nonetheless selectively limits how often she eats it.

Another account illustrative of the ways in which class location can be maintained through the construction of an other was made by Thomas when he was showing me the inside of his fridge during our second interview:

> 'We drink less milk than we used to and mostly what we drink now is almond milk, not rice milk because of the arsenic in it and not cow's milk … the cow's milk we generally keep for … for visitors who come and want … workmen find almond (laughs) … the stuff … they can't cope with it in their tea (laughs). They're like 'what?" (Thomas)

Of course, I cannot know whether Thomas had offered any workmen almond milk or what their response might have been. But again, this exchange is indicative of how everyday food practices are embedded with assumptions about knowing an other. Once again, class remains unsaid. But it is signified in the distinction between the cultural value attached to the different milks and the assumption that blue collar workers could not 'cope' with almond milk. The word 'cope' implies a struggle, suggesting not only that workmen would be *unable* to appreciate the aesthetic complexities of almond milk, but also that enjoying almond milk is itself a struggle. Importantly, similarly to my exchange with Des about his pesto, this exchange between Thomas and I about almond milk is as much about himself as it is about a classed other. The humorous tone of the exchange almost parodies the fastidious detail offered in Thomas' reasons for discounting rice milk and naming milk as 'cow's milk'. It suggests a self-knowledge that he understands his food habits could be interpreted as pedantic. However, this awareness is insufficient cause for Thomas to change his investment in particular foods such as almond milk because drinking almond milk is important to him. The exchange also highlights the dynamics around choice because Thomas situates his preference for only drinking a *limited* amount of almond milk within a list of different milks. That each milk comes with a critical evaluation, suggests that his choice-making process is well informed. I will revisit the theme of choice later in the chapter when I cast a socio-historical eye over the data. Prior to this, I turn to the narrative of John to offer some further thoughts about the classed other. Importantly, a 'workman's' potential distaste of almond milk can only ever be framed as an inability to 'cope' since he lacks the legitimized capital to authorize his claim.

John, the only working-class participant to be recruited into the study, had comparatively low levels of economic and (legitimate) cultural capital.

He fell outside of the recruitment criteria as it was my intention to only recruit participants who could be objectively positioned as middle class. Nevertheless, I included John in the sample since recruiting sufficient men was proving challenging. He had also kindly offered his time. As an outlier, John plays a key role in the analysis of middle-classed identities because he highlights the effects of being characterized as the imagined other seen in so many participant accounts. Research interactions with John were markedly different from the rest of the sample, bringing to the fore an awareness of my middle-class position. Here, he delivers a robust account of his household food practices:

John (35–44):	We buy a lot of like ingredients, you know like we've got coconut milk and pasta and stuff like that, so we can have stuff. We wouldn't tend to buy like a readymade thing. It would normally be the base ingredients and make our own ... so it wouldn't be like buying readymade pizzas and stuff like that. It's mainly we would buy cheese and ingredients and make our own dough, do it all our selves which is probably a bit strange, but ...
KG:	Is there a reason why you wouldn't buy a ready meal?
John:	It's just ... no we just prefer ... we don't like ... we don't eat much processed stuff as it is. It's not like a hard and fast rule but we tend not to eat the processed stuff ... we'll just cook something fresh. I mean it's not ... I suppose it is a bit, not snobby, but ... that's just what we like, so ...

Distance from processed foods was apparent in all interviews, but John was by far the most insistent, and in our first interview returned to his point that they do not eat ready meals or processed foods on ten separate occasions. Working with John's narrative in relation to other participant accounts, the frequency and insistent nature of John's disassociations with 'bad' foods felt in retrospect as if somehow I needed convincing that he and his family enacted 'good' food and that he was implicitly aware that his working-class habitus is discursively marked as lacking. On my second research visit, when John was talking and showing me through the food storage areas, his wife, Kelly, interrupted and remained present for the remainder of the interview. The extended excerpt here about their food cupboard illustrates the dynamics of the interruption:

Kelly:	You should probably be doing this with me (shouts from the other room).

KG:	(laughs) Right ok. So is there anything in the food cupboards that's like out of the ordinary?
John:	Em (pause) …
Kelly:	(comes into the kitchen) Em …
John:	She's probably best.
KG:	No cause that's the thing it's good to get …
Kelly:	I know … so there's the tamari, miso and all of that in there which would be … I don't know if he showed you this (opens cupboard door).
John:	I didn't because it was messy so I didn't open that cupboard (laughs).
Kelly:	So that cupboard like I say, that's got tamari and stuff which is an unusual soya sauce, and in that one there's Kashmiri chilli powder and stuff which isn't normally something that you'd always see … panko breadcrumbs in that one.

The wives of Neil and Gregg also interrupted during the food tours in the second interview, suggesting a lack of confidence that their husbands could show me the contents of the kitchen. This will be discussed in Chapter 5 in relation to the classed and gendered aspects household 'good' food and the construction of the kitchen as a feminine space. But for the purposes of discussion here, I want to explore how Kelly's interruption centres on the notion of respectability. All other participants interpreted the question 'is there anything that is out of the ordinary?' to mean 'is there anything that is not normally here?'. Kelly however, shows me the unusual and exotic ingredients in her cupboard that demonstrate her good taste. Skeggs (1997) shows that working-class women must guard against being seen as disreputable and explains how feminized respectability often focuses on cleanliness. Indeed, while John indicates he had not shown me the cupboard because of the mess, evidently for Kelly, showing me the exotic ingredients takes priority; they have more cultural value than having tidy cupboard. Later in the interview I ask John if the household is on a budget:

John:	No.
Kelly:	Definitely not.
KG:	Have you ever had to?
John:	No. I mean even when … when I was off [work] …
Kelly:	I think we're probably what I would say a little bit of a food snob.

This answer is in sharp contrast with the rest of the sample, most of whom drew on narratives of thrift in relation to their spending, as I will explore in the following chapter. In this interaction, however, my question felt like it was received as an accusation, and Kelly's definitive response is clear: as well as having good taste and knowledge about food, she does not curtail household expenditure on food. In other words, she does not fit into the imagined category of what working-class women are seen to be. Like the accounts of Des and Thomas, Kelly articulates an awareness that her food habits could be interpreted as pretentious. The difference however, is that Kelly lacks the authority to legitimize her performance of good taste because she operates in a social field which fixes the working classes as without taste. Being just one example, Kelly and John's narrative cannot offer a standalone indication of the ways in which the working-class habitus experiences 'good' taste. However, by drawing attention to their unusualness in relation to the rest of the sample, their narrative offers a counter example of how attempts to confer value onto the performance of good taste are experienced when one speaks from a devalued position.

To illustrate this further, I want to focus on two examples of participants playing with and transgressing the hierarchy of taste. For instance, when I asked if I could take a photo of her fridge, Jane jokes that she should have hidden a bottle of Coke:

KG: Right can I take a photo?
Jane (45–54):   Yeah. Oh I should've hid the Coke (laughs), no I'm
                 just joking (laughs).

Also illustrating this is Sara. Of the 343 participant photographs returned, there were only three images of take away foods. Sara provided one of these images (Figure 3.2), with the following description:

'That I thought was hilarious because it was … I knew it was probably likely to be the last picture that I was going to take and I thought oh how funny that it would be a takeaway. But yeah we obviously every now and again get a takeaway literally just from a place round the corner and I always get the same thing. I always get sweet and sour chicken cause it's just really good, really tasty. But it looks like it's landed from another planet on that photo (laughs). To be honest the colour is quite like that anyway (laughs).' (Sara)

Like Des and Thomas, Sara and Jane use humour in their account, providing insight into social understandings about food. A way of deflecting criticism from 'guilty pleasures' (Jackson and Meah 2019: 262), their laughter in turn validates the presence of foods low on cultural capital in their homes. Sara's image of the sweet and sour meal is hilarious *because* it is juxtaposed with a smorgasbord of other wholesome and homemade foods she had

Figure 3.2: Sara's photograph of a sweet and sour take away meal

photographed. Its positioning as alien to the household alludes to Sara's understanding of the taste hierarchy and confidence in her capacity to play with its boundaries. Through mocking the Coke and sweet and sour Chinese meal, Jane and Sara's accounts highlight how embodied capital provides sufficient markers of middle-classness which in turn can provide authority to reproduce and legitimize the hierarchy of taste. By contrast, even though John and Kelly know about the taste hierarchy, they are not authorized to play with the rules in the same way because their forms of personhood are marked in opposition to good taste. They are not authorized to speak therefore with humour and irony about processed foods. Eating processed foods is understood as a function of who they really *are*. To use the words of Bourdieu, this is having 'a pathological or morbid preference for (basic) essentials, a sort of congenital coarseness, the pretext for a class racism which associates the populace with everything heavy, thick and fat' (1984: 173).

Having set out the ways in which participants displayed an awareness of 'good' food through its relational positioning, I have implied that through careful selection certain foods are coded as legitimate, and by negation other foods coded as illegitimate. The sample appeared to implicitly mark foods and ways of eating which carry no value as working class while at the same time embodying classless identities. I now turn to life history data to explore how taste competence and recognition is embodied in key moments of capital accrual across the life course.

Coming-of-age stories and the expansion of taste

Aside from John, all participants were higher educated. Attending university and subsequently settling down into established households emerged as key moments in these participants' food histories. This is unsurprising since for most participants, going to university was the first time they started feeding themselves independently. Following Serre and Wagner (2015), the value of going to university is not just for the acquisition of institutionalized cultural capital in the form of a qualification, but also for the cumulative effects of a prolonged interaction in the specific field of higher education. Going to university brings a host of other knowledge and experiences such as adapting to different people and tastes, the conversion of which can help secure middle-class positions in adult lives.

Paying attention to early independent food experiences can account for these processes of conversion by making visible the extent to which habitus is durable and the complex ways that habitus embodies the marks of class through childhood. Bourdieu (1977) argued that dispositions are so durable that mostly they stay the same. It is noticeable that for participants who identified with middle-class personal histories, reflections about class in relation to their personal experience of food remained relatively absent from their narratives about the transition from childhood to adulthood. Already positioned well in social space, during this transition they were accorded the ontological security that their practices were validated through inherited capital. As such, participants mobilized their pre-engrained ideas of 'good' taste through a 'generative forgetting' (Lawler 2005: 440) of the processes by which these predispositions were acquired. By contrast, for those who experienced upward class mobility, several moments of classed self-reflexivity occurred in their coming-of-age food stories. For instance, I asked Mary, who was the first of her family to go to university and identified as working class, if she had ever felt aware of class. She recalled a time just after she graduated from university when she dined in one of London's high-end eateries: "I felt totally uncomfortable, like I was going to open my mouth and … I felt like a ten-year-old. I just felt like there were people in this place, like we just didn't belong in there at all (laughs)" (Mary, 35–44).

Mary's narrative reveals how she felt like a 'fish out of water' (Reay et al 2009: 1104), rendered childlike and afraid to open her mouth, despite her acquisition of cultural capital through university. Her experience reminds us of the dialectical relationship between habitus and positionality, wherein 'moments of hysteresis' result when individual trajectories incur a 'mismatch between one's (primary) habitus and the habitus required in a new field' (Friedman 2015: 131). As Bourdieu argues, 'practices are always liable to incur negative sanctions when the environment with which they are objectively confronted is too distant from that in which they are objectively fitted' (1977: 78).

Evidently Mary's awareness of the distance between the historical conditions of her habitus and the conjecture in which this particular food story was experienced, manifested itself in discomfort. Most participants who experienced upward social mobility recalled food moments such as this where their habitus was placed within the reach of their consciousness. More importantly, these occasions of disjuncture were recalled as anxiety-provoking. Illustrating this dynamic further is Jane. Jane strongly identified with her working-class upbringing, saying that in her 'heart and soul I'm a working-class girl'. She recalled leaving her childhood home as an unemployed teenage mother, but through marriage and education, she acquired the economic and dominant cultural capital to be 'bunked up the class system'. Next, she recalls the time that her now-husband took her out for a Chinese meal:

Jane: You know when I said I went out for a Chinese meal for the first time? That certainly, I did feel very like (pause) ... like I lacked so much knowledge and everybody else seemed to know what they were doing and I think that at the time I just thought, 'oh I'm going to ... this isn't for me. This is not my thing'. But then the food came, I enjoyed it, do you know what I mean? So yes, a couple of experiences like that where I've been places. Not so much now though. But I think it's all about experience isn't it?

KG: Who were you with when you went to the Chinese?

Jane: It was [husband], just me and [husband]. He surprised me, took me out for a treat (laughs), which was just like 'oh my God, this is awful!'. And I remember the first curry I went for as well (laughs). That was very much the same. Just like sweating looking at the menu thinking 'I haven't got a *clue* what any of this food is really, or what I need to order'. I think I had a little bit more of an idea with the curry, but the Chinese, I was totally floored by it.

Like Mary, Jane narrates a moment when she experiences a food-related 'moment of hysteresis'. Clearly an uncomfortable experience, it produced feelings of inadequacy: that she lacked the knowledge and confidence in her ability to 'play the game' (Bourdieu and Wacquant 1992: 117). Jane goes on to say that she now rarely has these feelings of anxiety because she has become more experienced. Consider this recollection in relation to her joke about the Coke in her fridge documented earlier. Far from an expression of discomfort, her performance in relation to the Coke is light-hearted and confident, suggesting her habitus is now secure within its objective conditions. That she has now learnt to play the game illustrates how the habitus can improvise, readjust itself and override its primary dispositions. In other words, while Jane's class awareness was a direct result of her position in the field being at odds with her inherited capital, the capital which she has since accrued and acquired over time has gradually become embedded in her habitus, suggesting that while primary dispositions are durable, they are not eternal (Bourdieu and Wacquant 1992).

All participants noted that their tastes had expanded throughout their life course. Most participants noted this expansion as occurring in conjunction with the acquisition of capital via university or travel. Although, as I have noted, the upwardly mobile displayed a heightened awareness regarding their lack of inherited capital during these times. Participants' experience of food at university varies across the sample. The older participants were more likely to talk about sharing food with fellow students living in same-sex accommodation. Many younger participants talked of sharing food with housemates, whereas others recalled living in chaotic environments, storing food in tiny individual cupboards in kitchens shared with up to eight other students. But while there is a variation in food experiences at university, participant accounts centred on the lack of restrictions they experienced in their food choices. Peter explains: "When I came to uni was when I started to experiment a little bit more with cooking and start doing things myself. Mainly because I was buying my own food, so I could therefore decide what I wanted to make" (Peter, 25–34).

Peter's account echoes previous research which finds that eating patterns can change across life course transitions, such as leaving the family home (Lupton 1996; McKenzie and Watts 2020). Elsewhere, participants talked about early travel experiences being fundamental to the expansion of their tastes. For example, Helen, who travelled extensively during her twenties:

'I don't know that my taste was much different. But I think my awareness of what I was eating is what changed. Awareness of (pause) different choices you can make, different traditions about eating. I think it's more of an awareness of the traditions of eating. I think in New Zealand in those days it was very heavily meat and you kind of just ate what was in front of you. Whereas having seen these other possibilities, I became at least more aware that I could make choices and began to start doing so I suppose.' (Helen, 55–64)

Helen's account is interesting because while she suggests she maintains the durability of her childhood tastes, she indicates that through travel she became aware of an array of food choices on offer. The subsequent widening of horizons in relation to food following leaving home to travel or attend university was narrated by participants as a trajectory of moving from restriction and lack of choice to abundance and diversity. Regardless of age, these food histories can be anchored in the context of wider social change, as the following separate quotes illustrate:

KG: Do you see yourself as belonging to a particular generation?

Ingrid (25–34): I suppose a generation with a very much more global approach to food. You know, I will go into Asian supermarkets, Chinese, Indian supermarkets and I will be quite adventurous with my choices of things that I will try and that I will eat. And in comparison to even my parents who you know think … it is that kind of like, 'oh pasta' and then you know various other … like it is a generation.

Gregg (34–45): Have my food tastes changed? Yeah I think they changed definitely. They changed … I suppose they changed with the … certainly with the availability of ingredients. So for example when I was growing up, you wouldn't have had coriander, but now you can get coriander everywhere. So like having Vietnamese or Thai or like Asian dishes that you would use coriander, you would be … or even making a guacamole, you couldn't do that properly without coriander really. So I suppose your … your tastes change because of the ingredients that are available for you to use.

Elizabeth (81): I'm one of the generation that grew up in the war and so was very influenced by rationing and all that sort of thing, yep.

KG: What about your children, do you see them as belonging to a particular generation? And has that influenced their food habits?

Elizabeth: I'm sure the abundance of food and the choice in food now has certainly influenced them, especially my older one I think. Although no, the younger one … olives, anchovies, you know, garlic, never heard of in my young days (laughs). Yeah. They've travelled too. They've both travelled a lot since … as adults. So, I guess yeah, I guess it does. They've had all these choices, they can make these choices, which weren't open to my generation.

These accounts suggest that the participants imagine that the widening of taste is related to a 'generational effect' (Warde 1997: 72). That is, they locate their experience of taste expansion within broader social change, which in turn marks them as different from neighbouring generations before or after them. Over 60 years spans these participants, yet they all draw on narratives of choice (or lack of) and the increase of diversity in relation to theirs, their parents, or their children's food habits. My point is not to dispute whether or not their tastes have widened as a result of globalization as Ingrid suggests. Afterall, we know that the food market is increasingly multi-cultural and diverse (Ekstrom 2016). Rather, I would like to draw attention to the centrality of choice in these accounts and suggest that the broadening of choices is a *necessary* point of reference for participants to make sense of themselves as consumers. Reay, Crozier and James suggest 'choice and the ability to make choices across a wide range of areas lies at the heart of white middle-class identity' (2011: 1). Moreover, emphasizing choice is also a way of situating the self in the field of consumption which values (and requires) the notion of choice and relatedly abundant options from which to choose. This point is reinforced by Warde who posits that since variety is a function of commodification, 'the desirability of variety, for its own sake, has become a central ideological precept' (1997: 193).

Warde (1997) warns against exaggerating the extent of change in tastes following the 1960s, since his research found that since then much has stayed the same. Like Warde, I found little generational difference between participant tastes (except Elizabeth, whose childhood history dated to before World War Two and will be explored in due course). Nevertheless, all participants appeared to draw on the notion of choice which, as their accounts suggest, they understand to be offered by globalization. But the greater *production* of variety does not necessarily mean the expansion of individual tastes to include a more diverse set of foods. While, as Gregg suggested, he now eats coriander, at the same time, he rejects many of the foods of his childhood. Here he describes a buffet his mother used to host at Christmas time:

> 'And then she would do ... and it became more obvious as I got older what I thought was sort of older sort of types of food. Like she would boil eggs and like slice them and then put mayonnaise on them and stuff like that and maybe 70s sorts of dishes that were a bit odd.' (Gregg)

While framed in terms of diversity and abundance, the adoption of new foods simultaneously appears to involve the rejection of old foods: Gregg now steers clear of the 1970s dishes his mum used to provide. As the next section will explore, the prevalence of choice and diversity in participants' narratives about taste speaks more about that which it excludes than that which it includes.

Restricting choice

All participants noted the particular life stage of settling down with partners and post-university relationships as being fundamental in their food journeys for facilitating an environment in which to cook and appreciate food. This is in line with Warde's findings that differences in food practices are more about life stages than generational difference. As Warde suggests, 'as cohorts aged, they tended to shift their behaviours towards some norm for mature family households' (1997: 75). In relation to this suggestion, I would like to expand on this further by proposing that there is something very specific about these narratives of settling down. For most, a key moment of being able to actively appreciate and do 'good' food was through forging bonds within or just after the specific environment of higher education with others who had similarly accrued cultural capital through university. Several participants were operating within economic constraints at university. But, by subsequently having a 'proper job', they were then able to combine economic capital with their acquired social and cultural capital (university and graduate social networks and gaining a degree) to take forward a consensual recognition of the cultural value of good taste into their established households. In this way, the mapping of participant journeys specifically including university indicates how class can enrich our understanding of coming of age through food. These participants carried economic, social and cultural capital into their 'settled' households.

As we have seen, participants often mentioned coriander, hummus, olives, and avocado in their talk about the increase of choices (coriander was mentioned by ten participants). Alongside the increased availability of coriander however, we have also seen an increase in the availability and range of junk foods and convenience foods, such as microwave meals and the arrival of fast-food chains in Britain. However, these foods rarely entered participant narratives, except as a point from which to enact differentiation. The second wave interviews provide some evidence of convenience foods crossing the threshold into the food cupboards, but their presence was always defended against with justifications of harriedness or indulgence. These justifications will be dealt with in the next chapter. My point here, however, is that while participants appear to understand that their tastes have expanded due to the abundance of choice provided by contemporary consumer culture, they only consume a relatively limited range of foods. In fact, participants tightly restricted which foods entered their households. Participants often pointed out the increase in production of variety in the literal and metaphorical food markets around them. Yet they also appeared to provide evidence to the contrary in terms of their individual choices not to consume all the plethora of food options available to them. Fiona's account illustrates how restriction and choice are conceptualized in relation to three separate generations:

Fiona: I didn't have any food choices when I was young I guess. I had to eat what I was given because there wasn't anything else (laughs). Whereas I guess my kids, it wasn't quite so strained, the circumstances they were brought up in. But they were expected to eat what I'd made them and if they didn't like it there was sometimes another option, but that wasn't the case for me. I did try to make them eat healthily, as far as I could, but then I discovered my son was swapping his healthy dinner for jam sandwiches (laughs) and something else (laughs). So that didn't always work. I notice my grandchild, it's ... they are extremely particular about what he eats. So in one way, they're ... he doesn't have anything sort of unhealthy. He eats a lot of berries and fruit and so on, he's just one, so he's just ... (pause).

KG: Just learning to eat?

Fiona: Just learning to eat. But he will eat what we eat. So if we're having, I don't know, if we're having ... well, we were having ... for breakfast we were having avocado (laughs) on toast and poached egg; he'd have that, just mashed up. So he'll have anything as long as it's reasonably healthy but he won't have cakes or biscuits or whatever else.

KG: Is that because he doesn't like them, or they just don't feed him ...?

Fiona: They don't feed him that, which I think is great you know; it's good. So he will ... he'll have pre-prepared kid's food when he's here sometimes. That's sort of pouch-y Ella something.

KG: Ella's Kitchen?

Fiona: Kitchen, yeah, sometimes, if there's something he really can't eat. But he is very easy and you know he'll sit and have hummus sandwiches and that sort of thing. He's very easy, but it's all quite thought about.

Grace makes a similar observation about her grandchild:

'When my grandson, the three-year-old comes, we'd bought him ... well I'd bought Coco Pops and ... well he wasn't allowed to eat them (laughs) – too much sugar in. But then I had to buy fish fingers for him, which threw me totally cause why wouldn't they just give him fish? So ... you know it's different fashions in food, isn't it?' (Grace, 65+)

Fiona, like other participants, draws on choice to understand her food habits. She notes she had no choice as a child. What she then goes on to say though is that her son and his partner are 'extremely particular' about restricting her grandson's choices to 'healthy' foods, such as avocado and hummus sandwiches. On one hand, she says he will eat anything, but on the other she concludes that her grandson's diet is 'all quite thought about'. Likewise, Grace notes her error in buying her grandson Coco Pops. The notion that grandparents provide treats for grandchildren is widely recognized. Curtis, James and Ellis show how parents often attempt to reframe this as 'spoiling' as a way to soften the impact of their challenge to their own family's food order (2009: 90). Similarly, Grace seems to challenge the rationale behind her son's highly specific instructions to buy her grandson fish fingers as opposed to fish. But what is particularly interesting here are the restrictions put in place with regards to Fiona and Grace's grandchildren's diets. While Fiona notes that she had no choice because there was nothing else when she was growing up, Fiona and Grace's grandsons have no choice *despite* the abundance of available alternatives. It appears then that the childhood food practices of both generations can be understood via a frame of restricted choices.

Personal food histories and mobility: pomegranate molasses and other preoccupations

To consider the theme of diversity further, I now turn to concentrate on the life trajectories of three individuals. This in turn deepens our understanding of the relational ways in which habitus occurs as a dialogue with the social world and an individual's life trajectory therein. I start with Elizabeth before moving to consider the stories of Maya and Des alongside one another. I begin with Elizabeth since her current food practices appeared markedly different to the rest of the cohort. Being born in 1934, she had clear recollections of post-war rationing, which she noted in her account about generation earlier. Elizabeth came from a 'very poor, poverty-stricken' background. Along with her four younger sisters, she spent a year in an orphanage when her mother was dying of emphysema. After her mother's death, at the age of 11, Elizabeth returned to the household and, being the eldest, was given responsibility for the 'housekeeping purse' until her father remarried a year later. He went on to have four more children. In both interviews, Elizabeth talked at length about not having enough to eat as a child, except on Sundays when she ate a 'very, very thin slice of meat', potatoes, cabbage and sometimes carrots, followed by rhubarb from the garden. Being born pre-World War Two, Elizabeth falls into the generation identified by Warde (1997) who is distinctive from the generations following, who were in turn heavily influenced by representations of exotic and foreign foods circulating in the public imagination from the 1960s onwards. This is reflected in her account about her everyday food practices:

Cook for my dinner? Well meat or fish and at least two other veg and either potatoes, rice or pasta. I have those and I always have pasta and rice in stock because if I haven't got potatoes there, it's like a standby. Another thing I have in stock especially if family are coming, for a quick dessert, I buy the Morrison's crumble, readymade crumble to do a ... and get the fruit from the freezer and make a quick crumble, because that ... the children find it more interesting obviously, the grandchildren. Otherwise, I don't always have a dessert except perhaps some fruit, or sometimes cheese and biscuits. But I try and have a bit of fruit, because I'm very keen on fruit (laughs). And so again a lot of it you see is not bought, because I've grown it. (Elizabeth)

Sociological research suggests that the upwardly mobile are more likely to display diverse taste preferences (Peterson and Kern 1996; Friedman 2012; Daenekindt and Roose 2014; Coulangeon 2015). Elizabeth, now wealthy in cultural and economic capital, has arguably experienced the greatest upward mobility of the sample. However, she also displays the least omnivorous tastes of the sample, the rest of whom drew on frames of diversity in relation to their food practices. Tending to prefer 'meat and three veg', Elizabeth retains much of her childhood dispositions and there is an absence of 'exotic' and 'ethnic' foods in her dialogue. It appears that Elizabeth does not prioritize diversity as being central to her tastes and preferences. Elizabeth's narrative underlines the importance of placing an individual's mobility in its socio-historical context, because her transition into adulthood occurred at a time when ethnic and exotic ingredients were not associated with good taste. Conversely, she talked often of growing her own vegetables, having things 'in stock' and not being wasteful implying that for her, good household food practices operate around the 'make do and mend' value systems of the rationing era. While most other participants talked at length about not being wasteful, my observations in Elizabeth's home suggest that she was by far the most frugal of the sample. For instance, her kitchen was in sharp contrast to other participants' dine-in kitchens displaying a range of prestige culinary artefacts. Figure 3.3 shows Elizabeth's daughter's old microwave which, given to her in the early 1990s, was her most modern kitchen appliance. Also, note the dishes on the draining board. She had said she has no dishwasher because she did not generate sufficient dishes to use it economically and preferred instead to only wash her dishes once a day so as to not waste water.

There is limited literature about food and social change (Nettleton and Uprichard 2011). But the data generated through my research interactions with Elizabeth illustrate the ways in which narratives embody specific socio-cultural eras, not least that her food-related dispositions established in the wartime and rationing period of 1939–1954 were hard to shake. Echoing

Figure 3.3: Researcher photo of Elizabeth's kitchen

Warde's (1997) findings about the generational specificities of women born in this era, the absence of diversity in her narrative marks her apart from the remainder of the sample. Interestingly, when I asked Elizabeth if her food choices reflect the type of person she is, she replied:

'(Pause) (laughs) I wouldn't know (laughs) … (pause) I mean I wouldn't call myself a foodie. On the other hand, I really do enjoy it and I like good food and I like going out to good restaurants and that sort of thing. But equally I could be happy with down-on-the-farm, plain food, as long as it has plenty of veg and fruit.' (Elizabeth)

Again this response is contrary to the remainder of the cohort, who reproduced ideas of individualism in relation to their identity and practices, and suggests an absence of the importance of consumption in relation to her self-identity.

Keeping the concept of mobility in a socio-historical context at the fore, I conclude this chapter by turning to the narratives of Des and Maya to explore diverse taste preferences further. In so doing, I introduce consumption anxiety and the effects of making mistakes on one's sense of (classed) self into the framework of analysis. Not all participants demonstrated an easy capacity to play with the taste hierarchy or to mobilize their cultural capital to legitimize foods. The following comparison between Maya and Des illustrates how cultural competence around food tastes, in particular ideas of 'ethnic' and 'exotic', is as much about *cultural* mobility as it is about class. This is based on Emmison's (2003) observation that cultural mobility refers to the freedom to engage with or consume different cultural forms. However, as I will now go on to argue, while the capacity for cultural mobility is classed, having resources does not guarantee the possibility of cultural mobility.

In our first interview, I asked Maya if her food choices had ever made her aware of class. She became very upset recalling a time when she had overheard her dinner party guests talking about food:

'They started talking about ingredients and the sorts of ingredients that they bought were things that I had barely heard of and certainly wouldn't be buying myself and I was thinking, 'oh my goodness, they are going to be disappointed by what I've got cooking for them'. And I felt very unsophisticated, and I still feel quite unsophisticated thinking about it.' (Maya, 45–54)

Maya had not hosted another dinner party since, indicating the long-standing effects of being acutely aware that she made a poor choice. Importantly, it is not that Maya 'got it wrong' but rather the lack of sophistication she felt about making the wrong choice, and her recognition that her guests would have been disappointed. Maya was aware of what was at stake through making the wrong choices. When culture (food) is integral to increasing the exchange-value of Maya's volume and composition of capital, getting it wrong is likely to generate feelings of embarrassment and anxiety about being unsophisticated.

The apparent uncertainty and anxiety which Maya displayed around her food choices could be understood by theorists such as Bauman as a consequence of the individualization and fluid cultural milieu of postmodernity (Bauman 2009). In our second interview, Maya explained she was planning to cook a Persian chicken dish which she had seen in a relative's Waitrose magazine:

'I picked this up when we were at my mother-in-law's house. She's got Waitrose just down the road so it's really convenient for her to go. But we've got a lot of these things (she points to the ingredients in the magazine), but we didn't have everything. But I've never been able to find this pomegranate molasses. Heaven knows where you would get that.' (Maya)

In contrast, Des' comment that follows about a photo he took of his fridge is an example of the levels of confidence and certainty he performed around his food tastes and preferences: "Oh inside of the fridge, with all sorts showing. All my middle-class preoccupations. So, I've preserved my own lemons and have got pomegranate molasses and loads of tins of tahini" (Des).

Maya's lack of knowledge about 'this' pomegranate molasses is telling when read against Des' molasses which he names as one of his 'middle-class preoccupations'. This appears to support Maya's first comment that her lack of knowledge about exotic ingredients had made her feel aware of class through her lack of sophistication which was actually a very painful experience for her. Faced with the 'omnivore's paradox' (Fischler 1988: 277), she is aware of a (social) need for diversity, but uncertain about what to eat. The point I want to make here is that Maya, despite struggling to construct the self-inventing identity valued in reflexive individualism, *recognizes* its importance. As her dinner party experience illustrates, there is a lot to be lost when your classed credentials rely on having good taste. Nevertheless, because of her classed credentials, people like Maya are less likely to make mistakes because they are supported through access to knowledge and having a clear sense of the rules. Many participants pointed out specialist ingredients such as pomegranate molasses, sumach, rose water, fresh horseradish, and so on. But Des' and Maya's contrasting narratives are especially interesting if we compare their personal histories. Both highly educated and trained in similar professions, they both possessed high levels of economic and institutional cultural capital, and they also identified that they were brought up in middle-class Jewish households.

I note the importance of placing consumption preferences of the upwardly mobile in relation to their socio-historical context through my earlier discussion of Elizabeth. The narratives of Des and Maya also allow for other forms of mobility as having an impact on consumption. While both participants started their life journeys from similar starting points, unlike Maya, Des' life trajectory entailed multiple exchanges with contrasting social and cultural worlds. He had moved (geographically and culturally) away from his Jewish upbringing and had also pursued a career which was at odds with his family expectations. Looking at class in isolation, both participants have increased capacity for cultural mobility which comes in part from their starting point of high inherited capital, according them with choices and autonomy to be 'active consumers' (Emmison 2003). However, Des, through his constant interactions with contrasting fields, appeared confident in his ability to mobilize and convert his inherited capital to display competency vis-à-vis diversity. Maya, on the other hand, appeared to have followed a conventional trajectory through life, such that the capital which marks her habitus appeared insufficient and *limiting* to her disposition to display and do the omnivorousness associated with good taste. Moreover, *because* the display of a fragmented and unique identity has middle-classed value, this appears to have produced a sense of uncertainty and anxiety in Maya when she recalled her dinner party experience. Most important however, and as we will go on to explore in the chapters that follow, being primarily responsible for the daily household provisioning of food, left little time for Maya to continuously search for new and adventurous tastes.

Conclusion

In line with current theories of class and consumption, this chapter has presented data which argues that individualizing structures are central to class relations. Contrary to reflexive individualism which sees identity as untethered from social structures, I have demonstrated here that identity can be connected to social structures when we pay attention to individual practices and dispositions. This is based on a Bourdieusian understanding that class exists twice: in the objective sense (through distributions of capital in social structures) and the subjective sense (habitus) and is therefore expressed and negotiated by individuals through everyday practice (Bourdieu and Wacquant 2013). Participant accounts of class show the complexities in class processes and the fractured ways that they experience class in relation to themselves. What emerges from this is the construction of individualistic identities through a play of difference to others. This entails evoking classed binaries and a negative other, which is implicitly marked as working class. However, the valuing of uniqueness demonstrated by the sample emerges as somewhat imagined. Participant narratives implicitly contain a form of collective class belonging which operates around not belonging. As Savage argues, 'class is salient in terms of constructing an idea of difference, not in terms of defining a class which one belongs to' (2000: 113). The sample repeatedly displayed a recognition that they can be differentiated from an imagined other who consumes the wrong foods. But also, as the next chapter will explore, the types of foods participants selected for their households are remarkably similar across the sample. Participant photos typically depict homemade meals involving fresh vegetables, salads, fish, pasta, rice, and couscous. Likewise, the types of foods participants restricted are also remarkably similar.

To understand these individualistic claims to identity, I have placed biographical narratives in the broader socio-historical context of globalization, diversity and increased choice. These appear to be the frames through which participants understand their food practices. They all locate themselves by drawing on a narrative of change and choice, regardless of class starting points. But choice requires access to and control over the range of resources which can enable desirable self-making (Skeggs 2005). Food choice is not experienced in a social vacuum and instead reflects the fault lines of participants' structural location. Through their class location, these participants are better equipped with the resources to engage with cultural forms to construct the valued individualized identities. By exploring these orientations towards selective taste expansion within a rhetoric of choice, this chapter provides the starting point from which to show how the sample negotiates 'good' taste through household relationships.

Finally, I suggest that while this is related to classed positioning, it is also related to individual biographies and mobility, within which the hesitant and anxious narrative of Maya can be conceptualized. Yet, Maya is not alone in her uncertainty around making the 'right' food choices for this particular social grouping, whose food identities appear to be built on not being like 'them'. When I turn my attention to the minutiae of food practices, I hope to explore this in the following chapter. Friedman (2015) points out that the upwardly mobile experience a conflict between rejecting childhood tastes and acquiring tastes associated with high cultural capital. However, the narratives of this cohort suggest that many participants appear to reside in similar positions of precariousness, although admittedly those with working-class histories demonstrate a fiercer rejection of childhood tastes. While all participants' palettes have expanded beyond their childhood, with excess comes the problem of selection. This leaves many participants apparently unsure about the ways to communicate their new tastes as adults as legitimate embodied cultural capital, *except* in its distance from processed foods. As the next chapter will show, in the process of carving an individualistic identity, there is an absence of belonging to a clear sense of food tradition, except in its distance from the masses.

4

Homemade Food: Individualized Processes of Household Investment

The previous chapter explored how tastes (and distastes) in food can be ways of situating the self in relation to another. This chapter looks at the enactment of food choices to examine how classed identity is articulated through doing. Participant biographies drew on notions of abundance and diversity in relation to food availability suggesting that the processes of food choices warrant further analysis. In light of this, I now examine the relationship between choice and the classed positioning of 'good' food within the contemporary food terrain. By focusing on practice, I relate the doing of choice to a complex and manifold set of routines, habits, preferences, and systems. I argue that the detailed ways in which participants choose from options to feed themselves and their households can act as a signpost to how they construct their sense of self, both individually and the household as a collective. Therefore, I explore the work done at a household level to manage choice, and the knowledge and skills which inform everyday investments. I scrutinize how these processes reproduce contextualized norms of middle-classness. This forms the basis for the following chapter, which picks up on this relationship in order to analyse participant enactment of familial relationships via food in the home.

To start the chapter, I turn my attention to the ways in which participant understandings of 'good' food are grounded in an attempt to '*decommodify food*' (Wilk 2006: 20; italics original). That is, through the process of cooking and preparing food, participants infuse food with personal, cultural, and social value. The value of food, however, stretches well beyond the immediate domestic work of cooking and preparing food, because it embodies a complex symbolic and material work of controlling and selecting the food which crosses the domestic threshold. I therefore draw on participant experiences of the marketplace to explore these processes of domesticating food. I note that participants' enactment and resistance of certain processes potentially constructs them as critical and discerning consumers. This is fraught with conflict however as the narratives of the most harried participants of the sample suggest.

The kitchen

To start, I want to first pay attention to how the kitchen functions as a central domestic space for the making and doing of 'good' food. Most first interviews and all second interviews occurred in kitchens. Participant kitchens were often open-plan and, while a site for the domestic provision of food, they were also clearly intermeshed with many other aspects of family life. Kitchens were clearly lived-in spaces in which participants performed a range of non-food activities, for instance music practice, supervising children's homework, watching the television, ironing, and reading the paper. The fieldnotes that follow, written following my second interview with Maya, illustrate how material and symbolic aspects of the household can be observed in the particular domestic space of the kitchen.

> Maya was busy in the kitchen while we chatted. She was making a crumble with blackberries from the garden as a dessert for their family meal later. She explained that they were celebrating her son receiving an offer to study law at university. I sat opposite her at the breakfast bar while she peeled the apples using a strange steel contraption. The kitchen was a hive of activity: the dishwasher and washing machine were going. There was a clothes horse packed with washing in front of the Aga, which she offered to move so that I could take a photo of the blackberries softening in the pan. (Fieldnotes following interview with Maya, 45–54)

My interview with Maya was punctured with sounds of the washing machine, the heat of the Aga was drying the previous load of washing, and the breakfast bar at which I sat enabled a casual sociality between us while she peeled apples opposite me. The breakfast bar bore signs of communal eating, highlighting that the flow of food in the kitchen extends beyond food preparation to include feeding and eating. I noted a weekly meal planner attached the fridge. Maya explained the planner served the dual purpose of meal planning and being an aide memoire for the household's evening classes and commitments. There was the letter 'P' written next to Tuesday. She explained it referred to her Pilates evening class, leaving her with a narrow timeslot to prepare and eat the family meal.

Several participant kitchens displayed meal planners which often contained references to non-eating activities. These planners were used by participants to organize food in relation to theirs and their family's lives, highlighting the complex spatiotemporal processes and dynamics of household food provisioning. Also attached to Maya's fridge was a photograph of her extended family. I observed items such as family photographs, children's drawings and postcards informally attached to notice boards and fridges in most kitchens. These material artefacts act as visual reminders of the household's social connections to themselves and others. They signify the multidimensional aspects of the kitchen as a lived-in space, acting 'to narrate the untold stories of lives being lived, those having been lived and those which are imagined' (Meah and Jackson 2016: 514). Thus, the social and cultural significance of this domestic space reaches far beyond the preparation of food, reproducing 'the *idea* that the kitchen constitutes the symbolic heart of the home' (Hand et al 2007: 675; italics original). It is from within this lived-in symbolic and material space that homemade food emerges and, thus, the household identity is conducted.

Within this scene of domestic efficiency and family unity, there was, however, evidence of Maya's frustrations. For instance, part way through her crumble she realized that her husband had bought the wrong oats for her topping. Later in the interview, she explained the domestic chore division, whereby she cooks, and he takes care of the dishes. She complained that he often neglects his side of the agreement and pointed to that morning's dishes still on the bench. However, read against Maya's weekday food practices in which convenience often takes priority in her efforts to synchronize her 'second shift' (Hochschild 1997) of feeding work with her professional life, this Sunday afternoon scene provided a window into the importance of homemade for Maya. It is well documented that women are disproportionally responsible for feeding the household (DeVault 1991; Brannen et al 2013) and I will return to this when I further unravel the conflict experienced by participants in juggling the antonyms of convenience and care (Warde 1997, 1999). The point I want to make here, however, is that on this particular Sunday afternoon, relatively free from the demands of her professional working life, Maya was able to construct a positive household identity through enacting homemade. That is, she performed a culturally valued version of domesticity through the provision of a family meal to mark the significant middle-class event of her son's future transition into law school. Domestic practices are integral to the construction of a household identity through establishing and reproducing the home through the fusion of social relationships in interconnected material and symbolic localities (Pink et al 2015). It follows then, that doing homemade can be read as an important way in which household feeders, like Maya, invest in the household.

The home operates as a multiple consumption site and cooking involves both production *and* consumption. All participants prioritized cooking from scratch which, as Ian summed up, is 'just so you know what's going into it, so it's easier to keep track of and know what's in it' (Ian, 25–34, nurse).

Figure 4.1: Neil's photo of his packed lunch

The concept of domestication provides a framework to understand how participants converted food, as a material object produced externally to the household, into something fit to consume within the household. Understood via this framework, it is possible to see how cooking and preparing food entails both the transformation of its material properties but is also a process of redefining and ascribing food with meanings according to the values of the home. Participants provided a range of photos of homemade meals and the processes of their production. These can be interpreted as reflections of their active investments to integrate food into their domestic space. Neil's excerpts about the photographs he provided of his packed lunch (Figures 4.1 and 4.2) show the multi-directional flow of this process:

> This is packed lunch. So this is quite interesting because [wife] gets up and makes my lunch every day, which is quite unusual in this day and age I think, to have wifey get up and make lunch and that's typical of what it is. Again it's quite healthy. So there's two bits of fruit, so I eat lots of fruit. There's a nice mixed salad. People often comment about these at work 'oh aren't you being healthy?'. And to me that's almost an extension of home as well. And it's made at home and taken into work and it's ... cause it's part of a relationship as well. It's kind of ... that's why it's quite important. It's very healthy as well. Full of pasta again, it's all kind of carbohydrates, stuff we think about quite carefully, or [wife] certainly thinks about quite carefully what's in it. (Neil, 45–54)

> More lunch, again prepared at home. Typical kind of stuff: pasta, a bit of sauce, nice mixed vegetables. That's got a four bean or a three

bean salad in there as well, so really you know quite healthy, prepared with love. (Neil)

Unlike other participants, Neil provided no photos of the processes of cooking, since his wife was responsible for feeding the household. Instead, he provided photos of his packed lunch, which, as he suggests, is 'an extension of the home'. His photos highlight the complex and multi-directional flow of domestic consumption *and* production of food, which for Neil seems to establish and reinforce the boundaries of the home through its connection to his outside world of work. The packed lunch marks the home as a site where his wife transforms food through (gendered) emotional work to give it symbolic meaning which Neil then takes to his workplace as an object of material, emotional and cultural display. He positions the packed lunch as a symbol of his relationship to the home, but his reflection that it is unusual that his wife makes his packed lunch 'in this day and age' seems also to position his packed lunch as a product of a nostalgic and heteronormative familial connection to the home. Being homemade in this sense is tied to particular gendered roles which express close intimacy, the kind of intimacy which is unavailable in market-produced goods or at least requires (feminized) investment in order to make that conversion. Neil positions the lunch as a healthy product of his wife's careful thinking, which is intertwined with care and love to produce a healthy end-product which he also recognizes is open to public surveillance and scrutiny from his work colleagues.

Having introduced the home as a site in which the material object of food is mediated and invested with symbolic meaning which can be read as reflective of individual and household identity, I now turn to consider the processes by

Figure 4.2: Another photo of Neil's packed lunch

which food is brought home. I look towards the marketplace as the starting point for a series of social processes involving resistance and accommodation and consider this in relation to the consumer rhetoric of individualism.

Beyond the kitchen

All participants valued homemade food. I have so far suggested that the domestic space acts as a hub for the conversion of food into a vehicle for 'family display' (James and Curtis 2010). This is through a process of investing symbolic and cultural meaning into food, in the kitchen, understood as a 'symbolic heart of the home' (Hand et al 2007: 675). There is a paucity of research which explores how domestic meal provisioning intersects with the marketplace (Marshall et al 2016). And yet the process of doing homemade stretches well beyond the parameters of the kitchen to incorporate modes of consumption outside of the home. The meanings attached to 'homemade' therefore can be read against the commercial interests of the market. Read in the context of participant narratives which centre on abundance and the globalization of food, it seems that homemade food must embody the symbolic and material work of making choices and controlling what kinds of foods come into the household from the marketplace. Understood in this light, this could explain the positive associations expressed by many participants about home-grown food. Across the sample, several participants were eager to talk about and show me home-grown food. This ranged from garden produce, such as fruit bushes and vegetable patches through to allotments. Since home-produced foods enable participants to bypass the marketplace altogether, home-grown, it seems, carries more value because it embodies a personal connection with the production of ingredients. Home-grown situates the self in the entire process of production and conversion, from soil to household plate.

Participants sourced food from a range of places: from independent retailers to large supermarkets, and as the following sections will illustrate, their purchasing decisions were motived by health, diversity, and quality. This, I will suggest, highlights participants' privilege, or to use the words of Bourdieu, their 'freedom from necessity' (Bourdieu 1984: 177). As a result, participants could construct an identity around navigating choice by drawing on classed skills and knowledge relating to cooking and feeding the household. To elaborate on this further, I consider in turn themes of thrift and navigation of shopping spaces.

Thrift: strategic deployment of economic capital

Several participants drew on discourses of thrift and austerity in relation to their consumption habits, for instance buying foods close to their sell-by date, bulk buying and checking labels. At the same time, while cost was important in relation to shopping decisions, many participants reflected that they do not have to economize, and quality was framed as the primary concern. Jane's quote here is an example:

'For some foods I think it's worth spending a little bit more. Like you know, I don't particularly buy cheap bread, do you know what I mean? But like cheap cans of tomatoes, I'll always go for the cheapest ones, cause it's just a can of tomatoes so in that sense, yeah cost does guide what I buy, but not to a massive degree I suppose … Do you know? There's money in the bank, it's not that I *can't* afford it, I just choose not to buy it if it's really expensive.' (Jane, 45–55)

This quote draws attention to Jane's economic and cultural capital which enables her to selectively take part in discourses of thrift: 'there's money in the bank' she reminds us. But Jane mobilizes her knowledge about food to suggest that there is little variation in quality in differently priced tins of tomatoes, and it is these evaluations about quality which drive her decisions to economize. Within these fine distinctions around value, there are some items, bread for instance, where she is not prepared to compromise. That Jane chooses to economize on certain things and not others, indicates her relative economic freedom as compared to shoppers with fewer economic resources. Furthermore, in making these economic choices, participants appeared to make judgements about what constitutes quality. This varies across the sample. For instance, Peter (24–34) said that he buys frozen Tesco Value chicken breasts since he only uses them in curries, but that he always buys premium brand coffee. Irene (55–64) said that she buys venison steaks in Aldi, but that she buys sugar snap peas elsewhere because Aldi's are 'stringy'. I will discuss tendencies to 'shop around' for quality as follows, but the point I want to make here is that while participants articulated varied interpretations about quality, their orientations towards the importance of quality was rarely compromised. Quality was the yardstick by which they measured their food purchasing decisions suggesting that motivations to bargain hunt have little to do with necessity. In fact, very few participants said they actively budget with food and the thriftiest shoppers were often unable to recall what they spend, despite demonstrating that they are economical and clever with prices. Take Julie for example:

'So yeah, going back to your other question, I've never had to budget per se, but I consider myself a savvy shopper when it comes to food, so I can afford to get something because I've kept an eye on other things, if you know what I mean.' (Julie, 35–44)

Prior to this I asked Julie how much she spends on her shopping:

'(pause) oh, I'm trying to think how much I spent today. I spent 18 pound in Waitrose and then I went to Tesco's as well and I spent about twenty pound there, so that's ... what nearly forty already today? During the week, it's probably five pound here and ten pound there (pause). 130? 150?' (Julie)

There is a disconnection between Julie's claim that she can afford other things because she has 'kept an eye' on her food shopping and her hesitant recollection of her recent spend at Tesco and Waitrose, a supermarket well known for being expensive. She then adds a further 'five pounds here and ten pounds there' to come up with a vague total spend. That she appears unsure of how much she spent on food again suggests that there is an absence of economic necessity involved in her decisions to be frugal. However, Julie accounts for her economic freedom, not by reflecting on her economic privilege, but by suggesting that she is a 'savvy shopper'. This performance of efficient and dexterous economic management implicitly reproduces the idea that it is possible to consume good food without high levels of economic capital, thus allowing her to maintain a position as distant from an unsuccessful other who fails to 'keep an eye on' their budget. Cappellini and Parsons (2013) note that practicing thrift, a middle-class disposition, is as much about identity as it is economics, which in the context of contemporary capitalism has a moral and symbolic dimension. Importantly, the practice of thrift carries cultural capital, especially when read in relation to public narratives of austerity, because it draws attention to an individual's ability to control the excessive consumption inherent in capitalism.

Many participants expressed a distaste for excessive consumerism. Charlie's account, next, invokes his propensity for strategic consumption by juxtaposing getting a bargain at a farmer's market with 'buy one get one free' (BOGOF) supermarket offers:

'We were at a farmer's market, a Christmas farmer's market and there was a guy selling game there. We got three tur ... three pheasants for a tenner. I thought 'well I know I can freeze two of them and eat one of them' so that was like 'yeah'. That's was kind of a bit of a 'oo there's a bargain. We'll have that rather than just buying one', cause we knew we could use it. So maybe that kind of thing, but I wouldn't ... you know the BOGOF and stuff like that doesn't kind of ... you know unless it was something I was going to buy anyway. So if I'm going to get a Lurpak Spreadable say, and it was on buy one get one free, yeah well why not, cause I'm going to use it. So ... but I wouldn't buy something else just because it's cheap, yeah (laughs).' (Charlie, 45–54)

Like other participants, since Charlie has economic capital and storage space, he is able to stock up and take advantage of bulk buying. This is an example of how participants can reproduce their economic privilege since they have the economic means to make these types of future-investing purchasing decisions. They are able to capitalize on and mobilize their resources in order to participate in the practice of bulk buying. But in positioning buying 'three pheasants for a tenner' alongside 'BOGOF' and buying 'something else just because it's cheap', Charlie seems to attach cultural value to the strategic element of his consumption choices and his critical reflexivity to see past the marketing messages of BOGOF.

Many participants frequent various shops to get what they identify as the best foods at the best cost. Aldi and Lidl were mentioned by many participants as places they shop, or as an acknowledgement of the growing trend for shopping for *certain* goods at these places. This is in line with media reports regarding the growth in popularity of discount supermarkets with affluent shoppers (for example, de Quetteville 2022), who are 'luring more and more middle-class shoppers with cheap but award-winning wines, dry-aged steak and cut-price lobsters' (Armstrong 2016). Given the media framing of these stories, I would like to argue that shopping practices which involve dipping into budget spaces, such as Aldi, are a means of performing distinction. Like taking advantage of *certain* bargains, it communicates strategic management of economic capital to make clever choices about what kinds of foods ought to be brought into the household. In the quote that follows, Thomas directly aligns Aldi and Lidl with Waitrose:

> 'But the fact of the matter is that there are some ... a lot of things we eat you can't always get at the German discount stores ... some marvellous pâtés that Waitrose do which we like, we just stay with those. So there's that kind of luxury item split. And I think [wife] would say if she goes to do a big shop at Lidl she'll come out with about 60 per cent of what she rather wanted. So yes they're great, they're cheap, and they're fast, but I guess for ... we sort of need to go somewhere different to keep up items ... [wife] uses a lot of herbs, fresh herbs for example, and they aren't always easy to get at Aldi and Lidl so you can go ... you come back from town from Waitrose with a stack of packaged herbs for example. It's ... it's a bit pick and mix in that respect.' (Thomas, 65+)

Although Thomas 'needs' to top up his shop with Waitrose goods, economic necessity plays no role in his decisions to shop at Lidl. Moreover, his comment that 'it's a bit pick and mix' denotes his freedom to navigate between shops, which can be found at the opposite ends of the economic spectrum, to select appropriate foodstuffs and to discern 'the luxury item split'. What is notable is that Thomas, like many participants, articulates a complex process of combining foodstuffs from different places. At face value, practices of oscillating between budget spaces and more expensive spaces span the conventional divides of the taste hierarchy identified by Bourdieu (1984). Classed distinction is still apparent, however, since Thomas has the economic freedom to roam between spaces to display cultural competence over a variety of cultural forms and attach value to his selective food choices in the budget supermarkets.

Like discussions about identity, there appears to be a recurrent theme that the process of food selection in the marketplace is via individualistic and strategic decision-making, and by implication, differentiation from being part of a 'mass'. Literature which focuses on local or alternative consumption practices has explored how notions of authenticity are embedded in the exchange between production and consumption (Zukin 2008; Spracklen 2011; Weiss 2012; Cappellini et al 2015). Furthermore, as I have suggested in Chapter 2, authenticity is marked as such in its distance from homogeneity. Cappellini, Parsons and Harman draw our attention to the 'wider (largely middle class) negative discourses of supermarkets as multinationals providing standardized foods for the mass market' (2015: 1100). An interesting line of enquiry to pursue, then, is how ideas of authenticity play out within and between the homogeneity of supermarkets.

Constructing identities through practices which engage with the idea of autonomous critical selection enables the presentation of the self as authentic as opposed to being influenced by mass-marketing messages. For instance, Des said: "Oh we've always liked going to Lidl, we think it's a bit like going on holiday, but now everybody's cottoned on to it" (Des, 55–64).

Des' quote is telling because he acknowledges the trend for shopping at Lidl, but by pointing out 'we've always liked going to Lidl', he positions himself as untouched by the trend. In the same way that Charlie positions himself as unaffected by consumerist marketing messages such as BOGOF, his quote implies a critical judgement around consumer trends. His analogy of going to Lidl with 'going on holiday' before 'everybody's cottoned on to it', can be read as an appeal to authenticity through the provision of himself as an 'intrepid explorer' (Cairns et al 2010: 602), who discovers an exotic other, in the form of the budget supermarket space. The food he finds there is valuable, not because 'everybody's cottoned on to it', but because it is a product of his adventurousness and willingness to explore across boundaries and seek out new tastes. What's more, Lidl has always been popular with shoppers who are low on economic capital. Hence the suggestion that 'everybody' has just started going there, appears to only refer to middle-class people, effectively positioning middle-class practices as the norm. But it is *because* of their freedom to roam across diverse shopping terrains that shoppers who are rich in capital can mobilize their 'pick and mix' consumption choices to demonstrate consumer competence by legitimizing *certain* products in the budget shops. Distinction appears to operate around shopping skill and innovation to select the right products for the middle-class household. Moreover, this strategic attitude towards investing in good food through identifying with being critical and complex consumers has the effect of locating the self as distant from the mass. It is through individualizing the experience of selecting particular foods from particular places that the performance of authentic subjectivity can be enacted. Choice and agency are central to ideas about authenticity through their play of difference to passivity. Yet, across the sample participants deployed shared classed knowledge about quality in justifying these practices. Moreover, while careful selection facilitates a performance of authenticity, choices are nevertheless made within spaces 'that are defined and bounded by hegemonic interests of commerce' (Spracklen et al 2013: 306). As Cappellini, Parsons and Harman point out, combining extravagance with budgeting across supermarket spaces is less about serendipity and more about efficiently combining 'legitimate, thus safe ingredients, which have been approved by trusted and delocalized sources' (2015: 1098). As I will now go on to show, this extends to independent marketplaces too.

Diverse shopping spaces

I have so far suggested that economic principles are not the sole operators driving participant consumption preferences. As well as performing distinction through economic skill and innovation to select foods, how participants discern places of consumption can shed light on how class influences their journeys across the wealth of options offered in the marketplace. Many participants either frequented, or expressed a preference for 'local' and independent stores. These stores appear to offer an opportunity to avoid mainstream consumerism and, therefore, the investment of authenticity into shopping practices. Helen's story here about her trips to the 'West End Store' is in response to my commenting on the bulk bags of spices and nuts in her food cupboards:

Helen (55–64):	Whenever we do go over there we would always buy … you know they have the best spinach in Newcastle and you know other nice vegetables, beautiful coriander and stuff like that …
KG:	Yeah, what is it about the store that you like?
Helen:	I guess it's the fact that it's owned by … I mean he's a bit of grumpy old man, but the old guy who's been there forever, is always there behind the counter, behind the till rather. People seem to … I just …

> I like the diversity of the customers there, it's kind
> of … kind of friendly, beautiful fresh produce, I just
> think it's a nice … a nice … a nice sort of … a nice
> thing to have so I like to support it. I'm a rather
> foolishly loyal customer (laughs).

Askegaard and Brogärd (2016) ask how people negotiate and understand the separation of 'real', authentic food from its opposite, arguing that we need to understand the idea of authenticity in relation to everyday practices of food provisioning. Helen says the store is 'a nice thing to have so I like to support it. I'm a rather foolishly loyal customer'. I am not disputing that individuals exercise their social and environmental responsibility through conscientious consumption and make sustainable food choices for altruistic reasons. There is, however, a tone to narratives about alternative modes of consumption that seem to stretch beyond merely exercising social responsibility. Like Charlie's recollection about the farmer's market, there is an implicit suggestion that frequenting independent stores is also about individuality and differentiation from the homogeneity of mass consumption. Helen's description of this particular setting appears to act as a means to 'do' authenticity (Askegaard and Brogärd 2016) through her personal connection with the process of consumption. Putting a face to the food that she buys appears to provide her with a sense of intimacy, longevity, and tradition: the 'grumpy old man' has been serving her 'the best spinach in Newcastle' and 'beautiful coriander' 'forever'. As such, the food that she buys from this setting is beautiful because of her first-hand connection with the diversity and the imagined authenticity therein. Furthermore, that she is loyal to the grumpy man appears to suggest that this experience is worthy of perseverance. In other words, there is work involved in differentiating the self from a block of consumers who passively buy mass-produced foodstuffs.

Other participants talked about shopping in Newcastle's city centre Grainger Market. Almost 200 years old, in recent years the market hall has evolved considerably from the traditional butchers and greengrocers originally housed there. Although the market is still well known for its affordable prices, alongside the veg displays and animal carcasses hanging outside of butchers, there are now 'street food' outlets, delicatessens and other specialist shops. I now turn to focus on Ingrid as an example of how authenticity and distaste of the mass plays out in several moments in one participant's narrative. She described in detail the kinds of foods she purchased from the Grainger Market:

> 'I think when we first started doing it we were a bit suspect about
> how much we could get but actually, you know, the veg and stuff is so
> cheap and fruit, especially this time of year. It's a bargain … we tend

to get quite a bit and now they have spread out, it used to be much more bog-standard basics but they've got a lot more deli stuff in there now so it's quite good. Like there's [shop name], the nice deli place, so they help if you need random stuff, cause we both like cooking so we have … we do tend to buy random things, sort of posh bits and pieces from there as well. But I think we tend to shop in the Grainger Market because it is so cheap … they've got a lot better I think. There's a lot more understanding of the … I think they've understood more of like what the market is and the Grainger market has got a bit more upmarket in what they should be offering. So, it's got a much better mix now.' (Ingrid, 25–34)

Like Helen, Ingrid draws on ideas of intimacy in her experience of consumption. She recalls her original scepticism that the Grainger Market would not be able to cater for her food preferences, but through the actual experience of going, she discovers that it has evolved from only providing 'bog standard basics'. Moreover, these gentrification processes are for the better, she suggests. The stall holders have 'got a lot better' because they understand now that the Grainger Market 'has got a bit more upmarket in what they should be offering', which is 'posh bits and pieces' alongside cheap fresh produce. But the idea that the Grainger Market has improved by catering for middle-class tastes has the effect of concealing classed inequalities. This, in turn, implicitly devalues working-class tastes. Now, the long-standing working-class greengrocers sell bunches of coriander alongside their cauliflowers. However, it is the middle-class deli owners selling 'middle-class condiments' (Des, Chapter 3), such as wild garlic pesto, at extortionate prices (despite taking advantage of cheap retail space) who are hailed as being responsible for urban renewal through the attraction of middle-class customers. And while a new batch of market-goers savour 'posh bits and pieces' alongside an imagined nostalgic connection with working-class local history, this 'culinary gentrification' (Potter and Westall 2013: 163) implicitly results in older market-goers being increasingly priced (economically and culturally) out of the market.

The fine distinctions made around shopping in particular places suggests that these participants attach value to a food's point of purchase. This was often done through emphasizing a personal involvement in the relationship between exchange and value, in relation to the mass market. However, staying with Ingrid for a moment, I want to highlight some of the tensions inherent in people's search for local and intimate market exchanges. These tensions operate around a commitment to shopping local and the resistance of aspects of local which fail to offer a meaningful connection with the purchase of food. For instance, Ingrid then went on to say that the working-class urban area which is local to her cannot provide her with 'good' food: "We try to use the local shops cause that's again what we're trying to do, but the local shops around here are pretty poor" (Ingrid).

While she recognizes the inconsistency in her commitment, Ingrid appears prepared to sacrifice her commitment to shopping local, if the local independent store does not meet her expectations of good food. Instead, she went on to explain that she travels to the other side of town to independent delicatessens and ethnic stores, which offer the experience of making complex and exotic selections.

To recap, discussions around modes of sourcing food for the household appear to centre on demonstrating capacity through personal involvement in the consumption process and making discerning judgements about what to buy, and where, to limit the possibilities offered by excessive consumerism. This has the effect of producing individual displays of competence around good food. As such, investing in the consumption process is a means to imbue food with subjective understandings of value and a means to offer up an authentic self, which is untarnished by consumerist values. For instance, I then asked Ingrid about her understanding of cultural taste; she gave me the following reply:

> 'You know good taste is about knowing where your food comes from and *putting some effort* into where your food comes from, I suppose is what I classify as good taste. Not necessarily just buying the poshest thing off the shelf, you know, it's probably about actually knowing … *making some effort* to find your food I suppose and supporting local … yeah supporting local farmers and things like that is good taste for me because it's like, it may not be the prettiest thing in the world but it's … it's got some history behind it or some background and I think that shows a bit more … good taste is like *making the effort* to find local stuff.' (Ingrid, emphasis added)

Conversely, she defined bad taste as:

> 'Bad taste for me would just be taking the easier option out and just, yeah buying a really cheap lasagne and not knowing where it sort of comes from, or not putting the effort into actually trying to make something.' (Ingrid)

The contrast set out is between 'making the effort' to know and find your food against not making the effort to be reflexive about the processes involved in consumption. Moreover, although the other who 'doesn't make the effort' to know or try to cook from scratch, is not fully unpacked, Ingrid's mention of 'a really cheap lasagne' implies she is referring to those who are low on economic capital. And, while the suggestion that it is 'not necessarily just buying the poshest thing off the shelf' has the effect of moving the narrative away from class, the emphasis on 'knowing' is highly classed. It presupposes a classed competence and commitment to being able to decipher the symbolic codes that can be found in foods which 'may not be the prettiest thing in the world', as compared to the homogenized mass-produced foods offered from the supermarket shelves.

Sometimes explicit, sometimes not, the idea of 'making an effort' ran through so many of my participants' reflections on food practices, as I will now go on to explore. I have so far suggested that processes of investment into 'good' food extend beyond the household into the market to control and ensure that valued food crosses the threshold into the domestic space. Keeping the idea of 'making an effort' in mind, I now consider the conflict between processed and homemade foods. This is because the idea of 'making an effort' has ramifications for the participants of the study who experience harriedness in the context of feeding the household.

The processed/homemade conflict

The negative positioning of processed food frequently emerged as a comparison against which 'good' homemade food is valued. While expressions of taste operate as distinction, expressions of *distaste* for my participants appeared to be an equally, if not more, important means of distinguishing themselves. It was certainly not unusual to hear participants actively distance themselves from convenience foods, suggesting that people who feed themselves and their families convenience foods are a powerful image from which participants work to detach themselves. During the food cupboard tours, participants often pointed out a lack of convenience food as these two descriptions demonstrate:

Mary (35–44):   All my baking stuff I tend to keep at the top for some reason. Then I guess condiments and cereals are probably at the bottom and then the middle bit is herbs and tins of tomatoes and beans and packets of things really. Yeah, that's probably about it. There's not much else that I buy to be honest, like I don't buy a lot of ready meals. So, it's more ingredients like chopped tomatoes and beans, rice, pasta that kind of thing, rather than anything readymade. Like … like even soup, I don't really buy soup. I'd probably … if I fancied soup I'd probably try and make it.

Juliette (35–44):   So we've got jams and preserves. We've got chutneys and mustards here as well. And we always have a good stock of rice, pasta, noodles, couscous, polenta, that kind of stuff. Cause we usually have carbs in one form or another with … with our meals and … and tinned food. We haven't got a lot of … of readymade food if you like. We've got frozen pizza because that's quite handy for a … for a quick dinner, but mostly we tend to cook from scratch because well cause I don't … I don't like the amount of salt and sugar and stuff that they put allegedly to make it taste authentic (laughs). But we've got, yeah tinned vegetables and tinned fish and pulses and things like that.

Within these food cupboard descriptions, without prompt, both Mary and Juliette note the absence of readymade food, which appears to be a reference point for enacting distinction around the 'good' food. At the mention of tinned food, it is almost as if both Mary and Juliette need to clarify that they have tinned ingredients, not tinned meals. For Juliette, the tins act as a cue for her to remind me of her distaste for readymade food and that she tends to cook from scratch. As well as offering few opportunities for conversion, readymade foods offer instant gratification. To use the words of Bourdieu, readymade represents 'the basely material vulgarity of those who indulge in the immediate satisfactions of food and drink' (1984: 196). The presence of convenience food devalues the symbolic representation of the home because it removes the possibility of building a household identity of 'making an effort' to be personally involved in producing the household's food.

Echoing Meah and Jackson's (2017) findings, there were processed, convenience foods in every kitchen I encountered. To some extent, this contests the participants' ideological rejection of these foods, suggesting a disconnection between their construction of a household identity based on a homemade ethos and the reality of their everyday practices. But this is evidence of the complexity and situational meaning of 'processed'. While there is negative value attached to processed foods, their presence in kitchens can be used to understand how participants negotiate temporal conflicts which impinge on their ability to do homemade. This is because, within the extremes of a polarized dichotomy, homemade and processed foods interconnect in complex ways; the real action takes place in between. Furthermore, not all processed foods were rejected, indicating how participants appropriate and invest in food as commodity to render it fit for household purpose. Again invoking Bourdieu, participants appeared to value foods understood as having the potential for the display of 'aesthetic disposition' (1984: 3). In contrast, processed foods which offer no means of investment carry no value because value lies in a food's potential for the performance of individualized investment. In our first interview, I asked Thomas which foods he never buys:

'We don't buy a lot of dairy, we very rarely buy a processed meal … very occasionally. I mean I can't remember the last time we had a frozen pizza or another other type of prepared meal, sort of … we don't buy packaged meals. We buy pulses, we buy oils, we avoid can … no we have a fair bit of canned food in, you'll see in the cupboards there. We have canned beans of various kinds and canned tomatoes and sort of stocks and stuff like that. So we do buy packaged sauces, typically on stir fries or … we tend to stick to certain brands when we do that. We don't buy sort of the … a lot of sort of the ethnic stuff, like the Tex Mex stuff or the spiced-up stuff. So we tend to add our own spices, and do it that way. We don't buy … we don't buy many biscuits. We like to have one occasionally but we have … there's some in now but we don't always have them in the house. We don't buy … ah, we do buy crisps, but they're you know, the expensive kind (laughs). Hand-cut, you know the kind. So, we don't have great packets and bags of crisps lying around the place.' (Thomas)

Starting from his comment that he does not buy processed meals, Thomas follows by telling me that instead he and his partner buy pulses and oils as if to provide a direct contrast with the effort required in using pulses as opposed to eating pre-prepared meals. Like Juliette, Thomas' specificity that he had tinned ingredients suggests an awareness that I could make incorrect assumptions about what kinds of tins they were. He then goes on to say that they do in fact buy certain packaged sauces, but not the 'spiced-up stuff', since they add their own spices. He is able to justify his buying of packaged sauces, because he and his wife maintain a connection with the sauce by adding their own touch in the form of spices. His conclusion that they buy 'hand-cut' crisps adds value to the crisps since being hand-cut denotes some form of personal touch, but his accompanied laughter suggests he recognizes the irony of being hand-cut in the process of commodification. Finally, that the crisps are not 'lying around the place' conjures up an image of laziness and vulgarity associated with processed foods an image he firmly positions himself against.

During the food cupboard tours, when processed foods were evident, participants provided justifications for the ones which required little or no work. Take Ed's description of his kitchen cupboards for example:

'Well again, fish products, a reserve tin of soup, ham and pea soup, fish … fish products, Melva, atun, that's … again tuna. Spanish tinned mackerel, caballa. Some olives, but I'm … I'm averse to olives now …

spices, baked beans, tinned tomatoes, baked beans, usually for when the grandchildren come. I can always give them that. Tinned anchovies and then seasonings for my oriental stuff, coconut milk, noodles, pre-done rice cause it's … you know I prefer to do it but it's … it's the quantities if you're on your own type of thing if you make … I think that's probably just … the difficulties … it's portion sizes.' (Ed, 65+)

Ed identifies the tinned soup as a reserve, the tinned beans are for his grandchildren, and his rice is pre-done because of portion sizing. However, he provides no elaboration or justification for the tinned, processed fish (which he names in Spanish terms). Like Juliette, Mary and Thomas' distance from readymade foods, the tinned soup, baked beans and pre-done rice need to be justified because they offer limited opportunity for symbolic and material investment. As such, they have little exchange-value and are insufficient vehicles for the performance of taste. In contrast, Ed's tinned fish can be positioned as acceptable since it does not remove potential for doing homemade.

Ready meals, imagined or present, emerged as a powerful image in this research. I would like to argue that this is because they are the epitome of the corrosion of real (homemade) food. Being the product of mass production, ready meals require no individual touch. They offer no potential for investment, and, therefore, no opportunities for conversion into an object of symbolic value in the home. They carry implications of passive, as opposed to active and reflexive, consumption. Given the overall distaste for pre-prepared foods, when participants acknowledged that they ate pre-prepared meals, they were clearly acknowledged as not requiring any effort. For instance, Gregg (35–44) noted that occasionally as a treat or because it is quick and easy, he might 'sling' a pizza in the oven. Likewise, Sara (25–34) admitted that if it were a 'dire emergency' she might 'throw a frozen pizza' in the oven. Through emphasizing that pre-prepared foods are out of the ordinary, and using words like 'sling' and 'throw', Sara and Gregg communicated the lack of care, time and effort required to cook a pre-packaged pizza, thus keeping its devalued status intact.

Elsewhere, processed foods emerged as objects around which participants could perform distinction through offering a series of justifications. Two participants mentioned that on occasion they would purchase a Charlie Bigham ready meal.[1] Ed noted that while he would never buy a 'Tesco Value lasagne' he might buy a 'premium' ready meal, such as Charlie Bigham, but that he would enhance it nevertheless:

---

[1]   Charlie Bigham meals are expensive and high-end ready meals. They are marketed as being handmade using fresh ingredients in small commercial 'kitchens' (as opposed to factories).

'Well if it was a curry or whatever, I would slice up some fresh ginger … I haven't got a pestle and mortar here, but I would kind of grind up some coriander seeds or … and cumin seeds and you know put those in as well to kind of (pause) revitalize it.' (Ed)

In acknowledging his consumption of ready meals, Ed offers two claims which enable him to perform distinction. First, he juxtaposes a Value lasagne with a Charlie Bigham meal, displaying his reflexive cultural knowledge around his choice of ready meal. Second, he 'tweaks' (Naccarato and LeBesco 2012: 35). Although he has no pestle and mortar, he imagines himself grinding spices to 'revitalize' the meal and paints a picture of himself adding his own creative and personal touch to maintain his meal provisioning standards. Even though Ed is eating a premade meal, he still offers a narrative about making an effort (to enhance the meal) and being a critical consumer, which can go some way towards dispelling any associations of laziness attached the ready meal.

Pre-prepared foods require little effort aside from being 'thrown' into the oven or microwave. Homemade food is distinguishable from homogenized market-made food because it is invested with personal work conducted in the intimacy of the domestic sphere. I have thus far suggested that the justifications evoked by participants about the presence of pre-prepared foods in the kitchen denote a reflexive awareness of the importance of making material and symbolic investments into the food they provide for their households. I now look towards the most harried of the sample to better understand how participants negotiate investing in food amidst conflicting household responsibilities.

Care and convenience: gender and time

Convenience foods bypass modes of investment. For my participants, it appeared that convenience foods cannot be used to maintain 'healthy family foodways' which require work, time and commitment to a particular set of cultural values (Parsons 2014: 385). The individual process of investing meaning into food for the household must be understood in relation to a complex web of time pressures. In view of this, I now focus on the female participants, many of whom juggled feeding the household with paid employment and a host of other commitments. These participants echo previous research findings that women are more responsible for domestic food work (for example, DeVault 1991; Sullivan 1997; Brannen et al 2013), and consequently that working women are disproportionately affected by time shortage (Hsu 2015). Unsurprisingly, given the socio-cultural association of motherhood with feeding the family 'good' food (Bugge and Almas 2006; Cairns et al 2013), this gendered distribution of domestic labour was particularly evident in households where there are children. Before concentrating on the gendered work done in the kitchen to invest in food, let us first revisit participant preferences to frequent diverse shopping spaces. Many of the working women in the sample noted that shopping is necessary and time-constrained work, a practice which does not entail perusing multiple shopping spaces as previously articulated by some participants. Layla works part time and cares for her three primary-school aged children. Her comment here is representative of this group of participants:

KG: Do you enjoy food shopping?

Layla (35–44):   Not really.

KG: No? What is it about it you don't like?

Layla: (laughs) Well it feels like a chore now cause, you know, I usually have the kids with me or something (laughs). It feels like it's something I have to do rather ... you know I would love to do the kind of food shopping where you potter round little shops and the market (laughs) and pick up things and smell them. But it's more something that I have to do. I don't, you know, I don't browse or anything cause I've got my list and I just buy those things.

Interestingly, Layla acknowledges and recognizes visiting smaller shops and the market as a preferred practice. However, she locates shopping as mundane work and 'something I have to do'. While many of the retired or younger participants talk pleasurably about 'the kind of food shopping where you potter round little shops and the market', Layla experienced shopping as a necessary chore. Illustrating this gendered dynamic further is Harriet, who works full time and is also responsible for the household shopping. I learnt she had timed her weekly shop in an effort to try and squeeze it in around other activities. I asked her why:

'I have to kind of think, well when am I going to do the shopping? Or when am I going to have the time to do the shopping? How am I going to fit it in? And every week I have this – will I be doing it at eight o'clock on Friday? Will I be doing it ... getting up very early on Saturday?' (Harriet, 55–64)

Like many female participants responsible for feeding the household, both Harriet and Layla shopped according to a highly organized weekly meal plan. Keeping the idea of domestication as an analytical frame denotes the gendered ways in which feeding work extends beyond the point of food preparation to encompass a series of networks and points of work entailed in the assemblage of domestic food. From sourcing the food through to the handmade processes of embedding value in domestic food, these female participants were synchronizing multiple time-space paths of themselves, other household members, their paid employment and other domestic responsibilities.

Returning to the kitchen, I focus now on the microwave to examine these dynamics further. Bar one, all participants had a microwave, and regardless of gender respondents were quick to tell me that they do not use it for cooking. As Philip (55–64) noted: 'certainly not for cooking a meal completely or anything like that'. Instead it was used to, for example, steam vegetables, warm milk for coffee and make porridge. Again, looking towards the working women as the most time-poor of the sample seems to be a good way of exploring this distancing to an object which facilitates convenience and the compression of time pressures. The excerpt here is Mary's response to my question, 'what do you use your microwave for?':

'Warming porridge up, mostly and occasionally reheating leftovers. Occasionally defrosting something. I went for a long time without a microwave, I've only probably had one the last three or four, five maybe years. Yeah not … like when he [her son] was a baby I know we didn't have one, cause we had the electric sterilizer. I know like a couple of people said to me, you'll not be able to manage without a microwave and I was determined to, so I did (laughs) for like two or three years and then I thought "oh I might as well just get one for defrosting stuff".' (Mary)

Mary is clear that she is not the type of person who needs a microwave, nor indeed uses it on a regular basis. Indeed, the ways in which Mary actively distances from her microwave could be read as similar to her disavowal of readymade foods in her description of her food cupboard. Sara's narrative here is remarkably similar:

'To be honest probably only use that [the microwave] for cooking peas and broccoli and that's just because you can kind of steam them. So I tend to just put them in a bowl with a bit of water and some cling on the top and it almost just steams it. But I don't … I don't really use the microwave other than that. Other than maybe to reheat the odd leftover if it's alright in the microwave. I tend to either do it on the hob or put it in the oven, and reheat it sort of more slowly. But yeah it's also … I mean when I was in London, our flat didn't have a microwave and it was … I managed completely fine.' (Sara)

Like Mary, Sara notes that she can manage fine without the microwave, and that she rarely uses it. The emphasis on time in her quote is interesting

Figure 4.3: Researcher photo of Sara's microwave with pestle and mortar on top

because she suggests that while green vegetables can be 'almost just' steamed, leftovers are better reheated slowly in the oven or on the hob. This is in stark contrast to the lack of precision evoked in her comment earlier about a frozen pizza which she might 'throw' in the oven. Moreover, on top of the microwave sits a pestle and mortar (Figure 4.3). This is probably a convenient place for its storage; however, it provides an interesting juxtaposition and visual representation of the homemade/convenience antonym. The display of the pestle and mortar on top of the microwave almost mitigates the presence of the microwave as a convenience item because it offers a contrasting depiction of the household as one which engages in time-intensive cooking from scratch.

Microwaves, like ready meals, carry imagined distasteful connotations of laziness and cutting corners. Through their association with convenience, they emerged in this research in opposition to doing homemade. Following Shove and Southerton's (2000) findings, as we have seen, participants voiced ambivalence towards the microwave, emphasizing that they (occasionally) use it to support homemade (defrosting and reheating). In other words, using this technology is deemed acceptable for striking a compromise between doing homemade and being time compressed, but not as a complete replacement of the process of cooking. This further emphasizes participants' commitment to doing homemade – even when harried, the expectations of feeding the household 'proper' food appeared to take priority. Yet, participants appeared only too aware of the potential implications of making the wrong short cuts. In the excerpt that follows, mother-of-four Carla details how she negotiates care and convenience to feed her family within time constraints:

'I suppose there're three things that I do that're not … I buy either pesto or some kind of tomato-y sauce that they're fine with pasta. But then I probably add … like if I buy a tomato-y sauce I probably cut up bits of ham into it and then I will cook some greens alongside it, so they'll have broccoli or green beans alongside it and … or pesto sauce, you know. Quiche – I buy quiche and just heat it up and then they might have potato salad with that and some … you know I do a lot just cutting up carrots, so they've got raw carrots, some … they all eat um sugar snap peas, raw, so you know as long as I've got something that I know they're getting some kind of vegetable thing alongside what I've got, I might just buy quiche. And then they all like the pies from [name] Bakery up the road, so that's my kind of naughty, you know … they are … they cook them there, so they're not … it's not like you know ready … ready … totally salt-induced, (laughs) loaded ready meal, but they are ready-done, you know. I've not done anything and that's … that is a quick, if I really just can't be bothered or you know they're going out and they're all eating at different times. That's the other thing that sometimes is difficult when they've got activities at different times. So the pies are really good for that cause I can just heat them up when they're … but then again you know I still cook some green vegetables. So we had pies last night but I made broccoli for them to have and some salad so it was … I just try to do a bit of you know.' (Carla, 45–54)

Carla, who worked full time, was a single mother with four children ranging from seven to 14 years old. Yet, it seems she must continually guard against potential judgements and justify her occasional shortcuts of using pre-prepared foods. She does this by placing emphasis on the fact that she still prioritizes health and repeatedly tells me that even though she 'just heats up' the odd quiche or pie, she puts the work in by cutting up extra raw veg and cooking broccoli. To this end, it seems fair to assume that the pies from the local independent bakery are 'naughty', because 'I've not done anything', she says. And this is despite the reality of her juggling the extra-curricular activities of four children while working full time. Moreover, Carla uses the processed foods to retain an element of homemade, such that their presence becomes diluted by other homemade components: they facilitate the negotiation of convenience to enable the provisioning of a meal as opposed to completely replace it. Carla very clearly positions herself on the spectrum of homemade to processed foods, in her distinction that the pies are not a 'totally salt-induced, (laughs) loaded ready meal'. Understood in the context of moralized public narratives around bad parenting, the decline of cooking, the increase in junk food and the prevalence of microwave meals, Carla's narrative appears to centre on respectability and competency by being able to improvise within time constraints to retain an element of cooking by adding vegetables so as to provide a quick and 'healthy' meal.

Here we see gender and class working together to reproduce and normalize a cultural rhetoric of women as the 'guardians of health (and morality) of the family' (Parsons 2014: 387). While some of the men in the sample cooked, in households with and without children women were in charge of the domestic management of food. However, there was a lack of reflexivity on behalf of the female participants about the unfairness of the time crunch on them as women. This is a powerful reminder of a form of symbolic violence which normalizes the association of femininity and motherhood with food and feeding. Indeed, echoing Harman and Cappellini's research (2015), the way these participants discussed the tension between homemade and convenience food, class was alluded to far more than gender. This is because legitimate ideas of feeding the family are based on classed notions of being a good mother. Moreover, this feeding work was not just an act of care, but it was also a form of identity work for these women who were very clear about marking themselves apart from the type of person who feeds their families processed, readymade food. Despite the circulation of ideas of individualism, or perhaps because of them, participants like Carla appeared to be on constant guard about 'slipping up' (Lawler 1999) in relation to the rigid cultural codes attached to being a good mother.

Regardless of how harried these women were, they expressed a commitment to dedicating and synchronizing time to maintain classed social standards around good food. Through drawing attention to the fact that they were time starved, by not feeding their families readymade food participants were able to make a kind of status claim about being busy and not cutting corners. This was via the ability to implement 'time-shifting' strategies (Warde 1999: 518), such as using slow cookers and bulk cooking, within feelings of harriedness to maintain social standards of feeding the family 'proper' food. Understood in this light, it is possible to understand why some women expressed guilt when they were unable to navigate the convenience and care antonym to produce homemade foods within time constraints. As I noted at the start of this chapter, Maya prioritized cooking homemade on the weekend. Through the week she used convenience foods as means to juggle her busy schedule with feeding the family. Her participant photos displayed a strong theme of convenience. Here she describes her photograph of sweet and sour chicken:

Figure 4.4: Maya's photo of sweet and sour chicken

'This is a sweet and sour chicken [Figure 4.4]. Another easy kind of convenience thing I would do but I would cook the chicken. The chicken I've bought, chopped up and stir fried it with ... I think I've used some stir-fry vegetables and made my own rice, but it's a shop-bought sauce. So it's a sort of combination of those things.' (Maya)

Like Carla, Maya's description of this weekday meal demonstrates how she has added an element of homemade into an 'easy kind of convenience' meal. She notes that despite using a 'shop-bought sauce', she has 'bought, chopped up and stir fried it [the chicken]' as well as made her own rice. She went on to suggest that prioritizing convenience comes with sacrifices:

Maya: As you can see what I'm trying to do in the week is use the ready meals, and convenience meals, as little as possible while recognizing that you know I go ... I couldn't possibly cope if I never used them ...

KG: Yeah, yeah. So do you ...? When you sort of ... do you try not to use ready meals then?

Maya: (Nods)

KG: Why is that then?

Maya: 'Cause I ... I worry that they're not as healthy an option really and they tend ... (pause) (sighs) they're quite often high fat.

> They've quite often, you know, got various preservatives and other things in them. I don't feel they're as healthy.

I am not disputing that some ready meals may lack nutrition. However, read in the context of participant narratives around pre-prepared meals, it seems clear that distaste for ready meals also centres on the ways in which they undermine the symbolic and material work involved in producing homemade foods. Indeed, even though Maya relies on convenience 'as little as possible', the hesitancy in her admission that she tries not to use ready meals appears to suggest that she is aware of the moral shortcomings of feeding her family foods which she worries are unhealthy, or at least 'don't feel' as healthy. Taking Maya's framing of foods as feeling healthy, or not, provides a useful point of departure for the following chapter, which explores how the process of domesticating food from the marketplace to the household plate is centred on embodied notions of what constitutes 'good' food. While participants understand these corporeal 'skills' as innate, through the application of habitus it is possible to understand how these dispositions are generatively learnt.

Conclusion

Participants displayed an ability and preference to critically manoeuvre through the food terrain to position themselves and the food that they eat as having cultural value. Together, these themes highlight the intricate ways that food comes to be domesticated via an embodied knowingness. The boundaries of domestic eating and feeding extend far beyond the space of the kitchen to include a series of processes which are temporally, materially, and symbolically interconnected. In this chapter, through the concept of domestication we see how food is mediated through everyday practices which centre on its transformation according to the cultural values of the household. In positioning themselves as individual and critical consumers within the abundance provided by mass production, participants draw on and reproduce classed narratives about feeding the family 'good' foods. These processes are contested, entailing both appropriation and resistance, and the ways in which they are experienced speak about broader relations of gender and class. Factoring time and synchronicity into the analysis highlights the complexities involved in the process of domesticating food, namely regarding striking a balance within care and convenience. The harried participants demonstrated that as much as economic and cultural capital acts as a resource in eating and feeding, the resource of time is also required. Those experiencing time shortage might end up feeding their families foods which 'don't feel as healthy', resulting in the gendered and classed standards of care being contravened.

Participants' food narratives appeared to focus on individual preference, strategic decision-making and self-surveillance. However, as we have seen, these particular research interactions established that these preferred practices and preferences are remarkably similar across the sample. This suggests a shared classed knowledge around food which operates around critical selection, valuing making an effort and self-control. As the following chapter will explore, this knowledge is realized via a playoff between both inherited and acquired capital. In understanding the middle-class habitus as a culmination of both learnt practices and strategic accrual of specific forms of capital, I will explore knowledge about what constitutes good food in the domestic setting. To this end, I will suggest that culinary capital is embodied intergenerationally to produce a perceived innate knowing and skill on one hand, and on the other, is acquired by through an orientation to being up to date.

5

Culinary Capital: Knowledge, Learnt Practice and Acquired Taste

Bourdieu argued that taste in food 'reveals the deepest dispositions of the habitus' (1984: 190). Taking this as a starting point, this chapter explores how taste is not merely a matter of individual preference and choice, but a reflexive accumulation of generative learning. That is, orientations to food are continually learnt. I look to the past, present and future to explore how the sample mobilized learnt attitudes via familial social relationships alongside a disposition to gather and accrue capital as a means to do 'good' food.

The participants I worked with clearly appeared to prioritize the strategic importance of setting up intergenerationally produced food-related dispositions. I consider how the parents in the sample construct narratives around the importance of instilling 'good' food habits in their children. This social training centres on delivering children a healthy and diverse spectrum of foods. Yet, there are tensions in participant framings of ensuring their children are open to all foods and encouraging a disposition to make discerning choices clearly emerges as valued. In an era where childhood obesity is often moralized as a literal embodiment of bad parenting, the ways in which participants prioritize the production of 'healthy' children can be read as a reflection of their identity as parents. To elaborate on this further, I look towards the household meal, since it figures in so many narratives as an occasion where participants seek to 'do' family. I demonstrate how the socially constructed ideal of the family meal appears as a backdrop against which participants navigate between controlling, managing, and encouraging diverse tastes via the sociality of eating. Building on literature which frames the household meal as an occasion for the production, and display, of family, I show how participants negotiate everyday temporal constraints to stage household meals in order to reproduce notions of good taste via the exchange of food in a very particular domestic setting.

Embodied knowledge

I want to start this chapter with a glance towards public health messaging to consider how participants make sense of and engage with health as embodied individuals and how knowledge is situated in relation wider discursive frameworks about the performance of valued identities through food. Doing so lays bare the subtle ways in which food knowledge is understood as self-evident yet also anchored in public narratives which reproduce ideas of personal responsibility and agency. On one hand, respondents positioned themselves as critical consumers. On the other hand, they reproduced the individualized rationale of health messages into a felt sense of what are and are not 'healthy' food practices.

Individual self-control and moderation through food and eating emerged as central to maintaining 'civilized' and 'healthy' bodies (Lupton 1996). Stories established by participants around health offered themselves as being committed to limiting indulgence through self-control and, as Linda indicates here, taking a 'balanced' approach:

'I think I'm not sort of extreme but I think I am quite aware. And I wouldn't eat too many cakes or sweets or ... I kind of ... it's a balance I think and I would have one cup of coffee a day, cause I enjoy it. I wouldn't want to not have coffee but I think too much coffee is not good.' (Linda, 45–54)

Elsewhere, participants used phrases like 'as long as it's occasional', or 'every now and then' in relation to 'unhealthy' food. They were all too aware of the need to exercise self-discipline, but as Linda's quote emphasizes, they distanced themselves from being the type of person who is 'extreme'.

Most participants noted that they pay no attention to government health messaging. But like Peter's quote that follows, participant performances of care for themselves and their families seemed to both invoke and resist public health narratives:

KG: What about government health advice? Do you pay attention to that?

Peter (25–34):   Not really. I think I probably cook and eat healthily enough so I don't tend to pay attention to it. I know there's ... like the campaigns like trying to get people to eat five-a-day and that sort of stuff but I ... even when I was like overweight, I was aware that I was overweight. I didn't particularly listen to those, because I kind of was almost aware that I was overweight, and I knew that I needed to do something about it. But at that point in time, I wasn't willing to do something about it and since then I kind of go like I've educated myself well enough to know what I want ... what I need to do to stay healthy and I don't particularly feel like those kind of campaigns will resonate very ... like they just don't resonate really with me. They don't ... they're not something that I particularly pay attention to. Even when I've seen like the recipes for them, the recipes that they would usually suggest, I've found quite boring to be honest. They're not adventurous enough for me to want to try, the recipes they suggest.

Peter draws on his embodied knowledge to communicate that he does not pay attention to public health messaging, because he eats healthily anyway. Despite having previously been overweight, he says he was 'aware', he 'knew', but he was not 'willing to do something about it'. But here lies a contradiction because since being overweight, he suggests he has educated *himself* and now knows what he 'needs to do to stay healthy'. Ironically, he reproduces the individualized focus of health policy which postulates that health is the outcome of individual choice (Gibson et al 2021). Drawing on ideas of self-control, Peter, like many other participants, refers to the five-a-day message, highlighting his awareness of health policy. He acknowledges this message, as well as reproduces the individualist ideology of public health narratives through self-monitoring. Yet, he understands public health messaging as somewhat irrelevant to him personally. His orientation know is naturalized, highlighting the unconscious workings of the habitus and the taken-for-granted ways that knowledge about food is internalized and embodied, and culminated in practices of self-monitoring.

Questions about paying attention to best-before dates elicited a similar reaction. Most participants said that they employ their bodies to make judgements about a food's edibility, for instance smelling or tasting, rather than paying attention to expiry dates. Similarly to Waitt and Phillips' respondents (2016), participants drew on embodied visceral knowledge to evaluate a food's freshness. Yet while a critical interpretation of public messaging recurred across the sample, it was voiced in contested ways and always related to participant biographies. I draw on Elizabeth's narrative here to illustrate this further:

KG: So how do you know when something needs to be thrown out?

Elizabeth (65+): Often it's smell or appearance. Well in fact that's my usual. I don't ... I mean ok I keep an eye on the expiry dates but a lot of them I'm quite happy to ignore. I don't ignore expiry dates of meat and fish. In fact, fish will let you know (laughs) but meat would too. Now that's something I remember from my childhood. After my mother died, my father remarried, and he was away, I had to cook a shoulder of lamb joint for the Sunday meal and we didn't have a fridge, we had a basement with a cage in it to stop the rats getting in our food and that's where the meat was, and I got it out. And it was looking green-y and a bit smelly, and I phoned an aunt and said 'help, what do I do? Can I use it?' So she suggested soaking it in vinegar which I did and then rinsed and patted it and then cooked it and it was perfect.

KG: Really? Wow.

Elizabeth: Absolutely perfect

KG: So would you do that now with meat?

Elizabeth: If it were just slightly, yep. I wouldn't let it get to that stage (laughs) and it was only a little bit … we had no money to get anymore, and we couldn't throw it out so that's what we did. Soaked it in vinegar for some hours.

While looking through her fridge, my question about throwing away food prompts Elizabeth to recall this remarkable story about her childhood. What is particularly interesting is that Elizabeth is clear about marking public messaging, such as best-before dates, as irrelevant to her. Indeed, having been responsible for feeding since she was 11 years old, best-before dates do not even feature in much of her food history. Date marking was only introduced in the early 1970s in Britain, and this was for pre-packaged foods (Turner 1995). Having cooked for 70 years, Elizabeth's experience of discerning a food's edibility is well and truly embedded in her habitus. But the point I want to make here is that Elizabeth makes sense of her well-practised capacity to manage the food in her kitchen by positioning herself in relation to best-before dates. Moreover, she notes that she is critically selective about which best-before dates she recognizes and enacts respectability through saying she 'wouldn't let it [food] get to that stage' anyway. This effectively produces an individualized performance of awareness and competency about the processes of doing food, but it is clearly socially located. I have noted previously that Elizabeth's food tastes are at odds with the rest of the sample. Yet, her orientation to household management is shared with several other participants, such as her preference not to waste (although admittedly her frugality far outweighs the rest of the sample). The final point I want to make here is that in the absence of her mother, Elizabeth sought advice from her aunt. In light of this, I now turn to scrutinize the processes of feminized learning around *practice* which emerged as important.

Childhood learning and food

Bourdieu argued that 'it is probably in tastes in food that one would find the strongest and most indelible mark of infant learning' (1984: 79). Since the concept of habitus encompasses a person's trajectory across space and time, paying attention to a person's journey starting point (their childhood experiences) highlights the durable ways in which dispositions are subconsciously internalized and embodied to form a 'logic of practice' (Bourdieu 1990b). To recap, these dispositions are long-lasting and structured according to social conditions, but they are not fixed. They can be continually restructured during encounters with the field which involve the acquisition of capital, but these modifications tend to concur with and reproduce the initial structures which shape the habitus. With this in mind, I wish to consider how food dispositions are related to the conditions of their production and how they can be adapted through the accrual of cultural capital.

All participant evaluations of past and present food practices contained unprompted references to their mothers. This is unsurprising since previous research has established that mothers act as reference points for cooking practices (for example Bugge and Almås 2006; Curtis et al 2009; Cairns et al 2010). Research interactions produced rich data about the food-related learning participants acquired through childhood. Particularly interesting is how on one hand, these learning processes were often understood as natural, and on the other, participants appeared to selectively disregard certain aspects of this learning while retaining and valuing other connections. The two separate quotes that follow are in response to my asking how the participants learnt to cook and indicate how early learning experiences shape attitudes to cooking:

Juliette (35–44):	Well, seeing her [mum] cook every day was definitely very formative and ... I don't know I just never questioned it. It was just ... yeah I think it just came gradually.
Ian (25–34):	Often when I was at home, my mum was cooking, I'd be talking to her in the kitchen so I ... I'm sure there was a lot of observed learning. (Pause), so yeah, I'm sure I ... it came fairly naturally. Whether

that was through the observed learning and then
sort of filling in the blanks with YouTube and that
sort of thing.

Juliette's and Ian's mention of the 'formative' and 'observed' nature of their early food experiences with their mother signposts to how knowledge can be learnt and understood. Both quotes highlight that food practices can operate through skills which have been observed and naturalized in early childhood. The hesitancy in both narratives suggests it is difficult for Juliette and Ian to articulate and recall how the practice of cooking was learnt. It is difficult because I was asking Ian and Juliette to reflect on taken-for-granted learning processes which operate as something which is self-evident, suggesting that their knowing is a result of a logic of practice, subconsciously embodied, 'internalised as second nature and so forgotten as history' (Bourdieu 1990b: 56).

What came to light as the research unfolded is that these early food dispositions related not to food tastes, but to the household management of food. As Ingrid summed up: 'probably my mum is my main influence in terms of my *approach* to cooking definitely' (25–34; italics mine). Across the sample, these approaches ranged from keeping leftovers, to forward planning (for instance, bulk cooking and freezing), through to storing food in particular cupboards. As Sara explained: "Mum always had her sort of baking stuff all together, so that … it just seemed logical … well I just haven't known any different, so I've done that" (Sara, 25–34).

But while Sara notes that storing her food in a particular way 'just seemed logical' because she has never 'known any different', her food tastes are not so durable and long-lasting. As the data presented in Chapter 3 shows, participants understood their tastes as broadening throughout their life course. Most participant food cupboards were marked by an absence of foodstuffs which were reminiscent of their childhood. Sara goes on to say that her tastes in food have developed well beyond the 'basic' tastes of her mother and are now 'adventurous': "She had very basic kind of tastes but very good sort of staples and things so I've sort of … I think I've definitely picked that up but probably a bit more, well quite a lot more adventurous I would have thought" (Sara).

Hence, while participants retained elements of household management, their observed learning about cooking skill was supplemented with, for example, 'filling in the blanks with YouTube and that sort of thing'. Accordingly, 'family food scripts' are adapted to incorporate new foods across generations (Curtis et al 2009: 84) through the acquisition of knowledge about taste. This adaptation of learnt practice takes place as a dialogue between the habitus and broader public narratives about the family and food. As the proceeding section will illustrate, this involves the acquisition, and reproduction, of a particular classed knowledge.

Accruing capital: cookbooks

Many participants actively garnered and accrued capital to expand their taste preferences well beyond the tastes of their childhood which they implied were limiting. Many participants spoke of an ongoing commitment to self-education about food. This was often around modes of diversity and health. I began this chapter by discussing how participants distance themselves from public food messaging. Rather, most participants talked about seeking out and considering specific forms of food knowledge, for instance through travel, blogs, newspaper food supplements and cookbooks. Taking cookbooks as an example, I want to consider how participants fused inherited food dispositions with accrued culinary capital.

Most participants had extensive cookbook collections. This in itself suggests that keeping up to date with specific food knowledge was an active concern. Cookbooks were often on display in participant kitchens, suggesting that these forms of knowledge are a valued investment. Some participants put their own individual stamp on recipes and tweaked them according to household tastes and preferences. Nevertheless, a repeated pattern across the sample is that using cookbooks is an acceptable means to provide the structure for the doing of diversity through homemade. The images here are examples from the samples' cookbook collections:

Cookbooks offer an alternative to, or at least a creative interpretation of, inherited personal food traditions. They provide a means for exploring pluralism in the kitchen (Gallegos 2005) and enable the accumulation of selective knowledge of international cuisine and different diets, be it about ingredients, cooking, or consumption processes. But, as is evidenced by this imagery (Figures 5.1 to 5.7), cookbook collections were remarkably similar

Figure 5.1: Researcher photo of Ingrid's cookbooks

Figure 5.2: Researcher photo of Charlie's cookbooks

Figure 5.3: Researcher photo of Ed's cookbooks

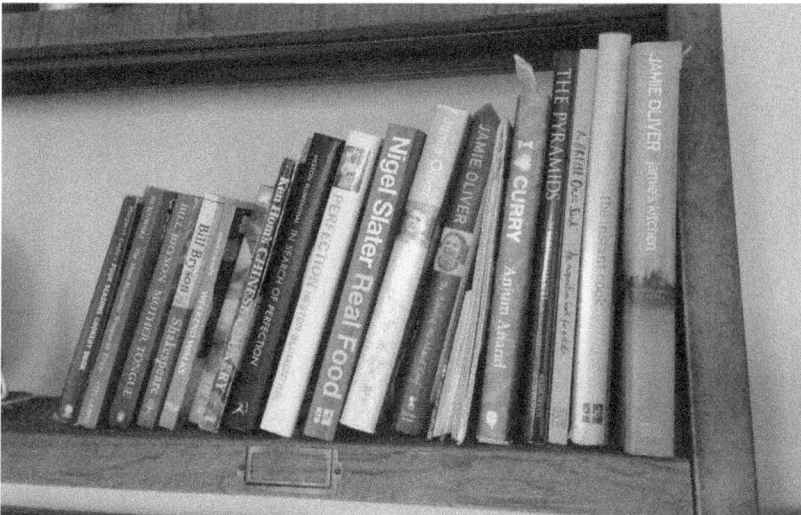

Figure 5.4: Researcher photo of Gregg's cookbooks

Figure 5.5: Researcher photo of Fiona's cookbooks

across the sample; authors like Nigel Slater, Jamie Oliver, Nigella Lawson and Yotam Ottolenghi were popular. The celebritized nature of the cookbook collections is particularly interesting. The abundance of books by television chefs such as Nigella Lawson and Jamie Oliver denotes how the rise of the celebrity chef in popular culture has been domesticated by participants. Part

Figure 5.6: Researcher photo of Layla's cookbooks

Figure 5.7: Researcher photo of Julie's cookbooks

of Jamie Oliver's appeal lies in his promise of saving time and money in everyday cooking practices – the everydayness of these books was certainly apparent in the kitchens of these participants. Books were often referred to by their first name, for instance, 'my Jamie', highlighting the intimate ways these television chefs are integral to the kitchen and adopted into family life. While participants reproduced the idea that food choices are autonomous and authentic, these cookbooks suggest otherwise: that their food knowledge relied on a commodified version of taste. Moreover, given the homogeneity of the cookbooks on display, it seems that the performance of individual taste preferences around food remains within a limited and narrow range; taste appears to be a mere variation of a broader middle class-orientation towards specific foods and ways of eating.

The similarity of these recipe sources extended across the sample, regardless of age, supporting earlier arguments that food tastes are less about generation and more about the impact of the broader circulation of trends around taste. Gregg's quote describes how his cookbook collection has evolved:

KG: Right so which ones did you first start using when you started to cook?

Gregg (35–44):   Ah that's a good question. I think probably the Jamie Oliver ones. So some of the earlier Jamie Oliver books are really good because they're quite straightforward. They're easy to follow. I like the methodology of the way it was sort of structured. And yeah, they were easy and it wasn't the type of book that had like difficult ingredients that were hard to find. So you could get most of the stuff in a supermarket or you know, locally or whatever. So it was fairly straight forward. Whereas some of those [cookbooks], they would ask for ingredients that maybe you wouldn't be able to get quite as often.

Like many other participants, Gregg notes that he started cooking with basic books which are 'easy to follow' and moved on to more complex books containing difficult-to-source ingredients. This points to the ways in which skill develops over time through the practice of cooking, the deployment of which is informed by the accrual of culinary knowledge, which itself relates to the circulation of ideas about diversity. Interestingly, the cookbooks he refers to as requiring hard-to-source ingredients comprise the main section of his and his partner's 'joint library'. These were either bought together or gifted from friends. This again confirms my earlier point, and that of Warde (1997), that ideas of good food are more about the specific life stage of settling down into family households, which in this case was directly following university. It also supports themes discussed previously that achieving household 'good' food extends well beyond the kitchen to include external consumption processes. Echoing findings by Cappellini and Parsons (2014), Gregg notes that his cookbook collection has evolved to focus on sourcing ingredients as opposed to simply cooking, suggesting that culinary skill is displayed through selecting the right products. Hence, within this coming-of-age story through cookbooks, the theme of sourcing and finding amidst diversity emerges as valued. Moreover, given the sample's distancing from childhood tastes and penchant for diversity, it appears that commodified culinary knowledge, for instance cookbooks, is a *necessary* source of cultural capital for the appreciation of and performance of good taste.

Alongside a range of contemporary cookbooks, other participants also showed me ageing cookbooks. These often acted as emotional connections to childhood histories, as Des description of his cookbook collection illustrates:

'Some of them have sentimental value, like the Middle Eastern Cookbook. That is … I bought new (laughs). It is well used and I think I've had it for … for years … I believe it's a classic but it's rarely … rarely been printed … the Cooking the Jewish Way we had that … whether that was my mother's … I've actually got a couple of my mother's cookbooks but they're in like a box somewhere upstairs.' (Des, 55–64)

Des' comment highlights that cookbooks are not merely classed sources of culinary knowledge. They have an emotional value too. This seems important to Des who talked often about using food to retain his connections to his Jewish heritage and passing it down to his children. In a sense, most participant cookbook collections display evidence of a hybrid relationship to tradition. On one hand, the participant's shelves (and kitchens) displayed inherited books and sentimental connections to childhood and traditions; on the other, they were awash with items sourced from the global marketplace. For instance, old recipe books containing handwritten notes by mothers and grandmothers could be found alongside contemporary cookbooks. But while the homogenous range of cookbooks displayed in the kitchens I visited is suggestive of a class-specific knowledge source, so too is the shared commitment to gathering and accumulating specific forms of knowledge. I do not wish to make light of the emotional value of intergenerational connection, but it could be argued that a commitment to integrating certain types of knowledge reflective of familial relationships and histories with newfound knowledge also denotes distinction. This is because the customized cookbook collections and personalized recipe sources are all socially approved by commodified cooks, certain media outlets or indeed specific family relationships. Whether intentional or not, they add richness and individuality to the collection of culinary knowledge which is used to feed households and visitors. Moreover, herein lies a conflict because while we saw in Chapter 3 that participants narrated biographies of leaving home and breaking away from their childhood tastes, they did in fact take selective aspects of their childhood into their adult households.

Culinary artefacts such as cookbooks enabled participants to situate themselves and their families through retaining memories. They also operated, in part, as a means of looking to the future. Many of the participants with adult-aged children noted that they had ensured that their children left home with well-established food habits. For instance, Fiona's participant photo of a pan of lentil soup (Figure 5.8) and accompanying explanation can be read as representative of the way food can be a means to bridge past and future generations:

Fiona (65+):   This is just soup, lentil soup. That is a sort of … it's my mother's recipe actually (laughs).

KG: Oh, is it?

Fiona: Yeah. And the kids before they went to university that is the one thing they could make, lentil soup (laughs). It's really easy, but it's really nice.

Des had said that when his daughter left home for university, he made a recipe book and spice box for her. In the same passage, he also explained that he had recently bought some wurst from Brick Lane:

Des: It's not very nice actually to be honest (laughs). But it's a sort of … it's a taste that's been there as long as I can remember, so I think it's about holding on to a culture that I had, but also creating a culture. So in some ways still we have a sort of culture … it's also about being able to pass on things. So both of the children, they have recipes. They say 'how do you make your curries?' and [son] would say 'oh I've been making hummus and it's like your hummus now' and [daughter] said um … I met her in London yesterday just for breakfast and she said 'well I tried your pinto baked beans' (laughs) and I think … that's nice that you've got that sense of connection. So it binds us, that's a …

KG: Hmm-mm, so it's not just the eating together?

Des: It's not just the eating together it's about the recipes and the … I think it's full of meaning, and it's a sense of feeling there's a tradition, some of which are old traditions and some of which are sort of new reinterpreted traditions and some are new ones.

Food can operate as a vehicle for belonging (Abbots 2016), both as a means of binding participants to their personal heritage and as a means

Figure 5.8: Fiona's photo of her mother's lentil soup

of anchoring their children into a family history. Read in relation to participant biographies, this raises a conflict since these participants appear very clear in marking their adult tastes apart from those of their childhood. For instance, Des no longer observes a kosher diet and Fiona previously noted that the food of her childhood was 'plain and unseasoned'. Hence, they seem selective about which tastes to retain and pass on. Moreover, this is not always to do with the physical taste of food. Indeed, Des appreciates the taste of the wurst, not because of its physical properties, but because it represents a taste of his past; it provides him with a sense of place anchored in familial bonds. As Des proposes, tradition is reinvented to ensure its survival into the present and future. He notes that there is a 'sense of feeling there is a tradition', implying that tradition is not inherent in food but that food operates as a vehicle for the enactment of tradition. Finally, there is a marked difference between Des' and Fiona's reflections around the transmission of food traditions to their children. Fiona prioritized ensuring that her children could feed themselves something 'easy' but 'nice', compared to Des who displays pride in his children being driven to tap into his culinary knowledge and creativity. This observation provides a starting point from which to consider again the importance of gender within the reflexive accumulation of food-related learning.

By paying attention to the ways in which participants engage with culinary knowledge it is apparent that there is another layer operating behind practice which relates to gendered generational connections. These connections function around the management of food. For instance, many female participants had well-thumbed copies of Delia Smith's *Complete Illustrated Cookery Course* (Smith 1989), a British best-selling cookbook. Delia Smith's popularity has been compared to Mrs Beeton, who was used by half of all British housewives in 1930s (Spencer 2002). She is well known for providing basic practical guidance about cooking traditional British cuisine as well as novel recipes. For the participants at the younger end of the age spectrum, copies of Delia were often taken from their mothers. For those at the older end of the spectrum, some were on their second or third copy. Across all ages, narratives about Delia Smith foregrounded household management. For instance, her books were described as 'really reliable' (Juliette), 'my failsafe' (Maya) and 'sort of reference books' (Linda). Taking this observation as a starting point, I now go on to consider the role of gender in domestic feeding in the context of household management.

Femininity and feeding

Ten of the 16 female participants talked of collecting recipes in folders, scrapbooks or notebooks. None of the 11 male participants did. These self-produced culinary sources contained recipes cut out from magazines, printouts from the internet and handwritten recipes from female connections such as mothers, grandmothers and (female) friends. These folders can be read, not just as cooking manuals, but as markers of biography symbolizing and narrating emotional connections across female generations. To illustrate further, I draw on separate conversations with Sara and Juliette, which occurred while we were looking through recipe folders.

Sara: This is just like my little rubbish folder that I've … if people give me recipes I just shove them in. Oh that was my mum's. She wrote that … she wrote that out when she was in hospital.

KG: Did she?

Sara: For my brother, yeah. Those are just ones that I ripped out of magazines and stuff. Yeah, she …

KG: Do you mind if I just take a picture? [Figure 5.9]

Sara: Yeah she em … cause I mean she … like I said before she taught me to cook and I was always in the kitchen. But my brother, well he's still a bit rubbish, so she wrote it down and I just stole it (laughs) and kept it. And that's just for a really nice carrot cake recipe and that's [husband]'s nan, who just turned 90 and she wrote that down.

In a separate conversation with Juliette, she noted:

So some are handwritten. That's my mum's handwriting …and yeah so I've got things I've cut out [Figure 5.10]. That's something my mum wrote, somewhere I've got one my grandma wrote as well. So some of them are there for sentimental reasons as much as anything. And yes it's … it's rather full as you can see (laughs) … and that's my savoury recipes folder and then I've got a pudding and cake folder as well (she gets more folders out) which is even worse because it's just got bits and bobs everywhere. So yeah so again it's … yeah things that I cut out, things that were written down.

Theophano notes that the generational sharing of culinary knowledge through the physical artefact of the cookbook functions as a token of female kin, providing a window into the lives of former female generations

Figure 5.9: Researcher photo of Sara's mother's spaghetti bolognaise recipe

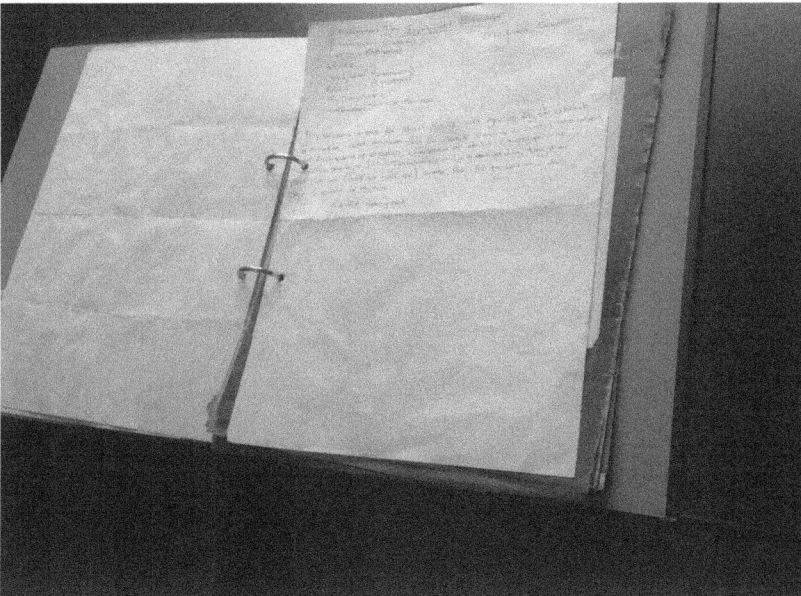

Figure 5.10: Researcher photo of Juliette's recipe folder showing her mother's handwriting alongside a recipe cut out of a magazine

(2002: 8). Consistent with that, the recipe folders just shown reflect participants' biographies and narrate a story about their family, its character and the types of relationships it offers. Acting as an 'intergenerational family script' (Curtis et al 2009: 83), the folders represent a sense of coherence that persists across the generations. For instance, although Sara's large cookbook collection offers several spaghetti bolognaise recipes, her mother's simple handwritten spaghetti bolognaise recipe seems to carry more value because it acts as a first-hand representation and connection to her past. It could be that this recipe acts as an important claim to belonging, since participant narratives locate themselves in an ever-shifting and fragmented social world. As Warde notes, 'customary dishes are a source of security, certainty and are often represented as emotionally gratifying' (1997: 67–68). Likewise, Juliette's folder contains handwritten recipes by her mother and grandmother. The folder, which is one of many, is presented like a scrapbook containing carefully arranged recipes. Older recipes passed down through generations are presented alongside contemporary recipes from magazines or the internet. The juxtaposition of these recipes can be read as a symbolic representation of the ways in which Juliette retains elements of her personal history while also actively embedding the habitus with new sources of culinary knowledge. Finally, there is an overall dominance of women telling these stories even though these stories are developed, enhanced, and changed over time. This is both within the passed down recipes found in the folders, as well as the female participants themselves communicating with me as a female researcher.

It is important to point out that not all personal recipe folders contained these sorts of generational connections. As I have indicated, all participants positioned their mothers as an important reference point for their current cooking practices. Some participants noted that their mothers provided good homemade foods, but that their own tastes have since expanded. Other participants situated themselves in complete opposition to their mothers. For instance:

'But my mum would always do the same meal, like Monday is liver and rice day, Tuesday spaghetti bolognaise. It was always the same when my mum was cooking because she didn't have a very wide repertoire but then at the weekend my dad would cook something completely new, completely amazing. He would often do ... I remember him doing like a Chinese banquet sometimes on a Saturday night with ... cooking everything from scratch, doing lots of things ... just cause he enjoyed doing it so much and I remember helping him from a really early age to do those sorts of things. So I do remember my dad introducing us to quite a lot of new foods.' (Layla, 35–44)

There are two interrelated points of interest here. First is that Layla distances herself from her mother's style of household management. Second is the comparison of her father's role in household feeding to that of her mother. I will address each point in turn. Like her mother, Layla managed the weekly feeding of her household, which consists of her husband and three young children. Like several participants, she dissociates herself from her mother's weekly cyclical meal pattern. While participants retained some aspects of a disposition, such as bulk cooking, this repetitive style of managing mundane feeding work was not practiced by any participants. Instead, they emphasized variation across several weeks, through the provision of a mix of new dishes and family favourites. That is, there remains a recognition of the importance of feeding the household 'good' food, but the temporal routines through which 'good' food is done are revised because the weekly meal pattern that for some participants was characteristic of their upbringing cannot offer the contemporary requirement for variety and fluidity. Thus, the inherited (gendered) propensity to manage food persists, but because tastes are revised, the management of food needs to be adapted to incorporate diversity. Nevertheless, the ideological value of doing family through the feminized delivery of 'good' food remains intact, which these recipe folders suggest. Moreover, many female participants were operating within fragmented and harried timespaces to provide a varied menu based on the fusion of contemporary and traditional knowledge, as I will now go on to explore.

There are no handwritten recipes from her mother in Layla's notebooks. She had several, dating back to her university days, containing recipes jotted down from leaflets, magazines, and cookbooks (Figure 5.11). I asked her if she still used the notebooks:

> 'I still would yeah. Cause I think (pause) … see I was looking back through this the other day because I was looking for a specific recipe that I cooked and that my husband really liked and I thought 'oh I've not done that one in ages. That was always a really good recipe'. And then there was … there are others in here that I've never tried. But most of the ones in there (Figures 5.11 and 5.12) I've tried. And what I tend to do now is I only write the recipe down if I've tried it and it's been a success and particularly with this book now, post-children, is like ones that I've tried with the children and they like and then I think 'I must remember to cook that again cause everybody ate it' (laughs).' (Layla)

At the back of the book there were the lists as seen in Figure 5.12.

Figure 5.11: Researcher photo of Layla's recipe folder showing 'My best loadsa veg bolognaise' and 'Singapore noodles'

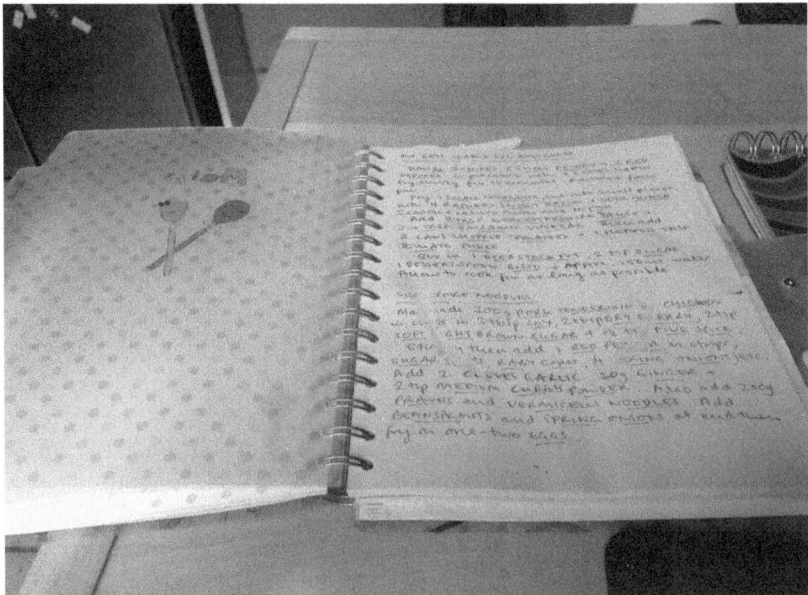

Figure 5.12: Researcher photo showing Layla's 'Quick meal ideas'; page behind: 'Meals that work for whole family'

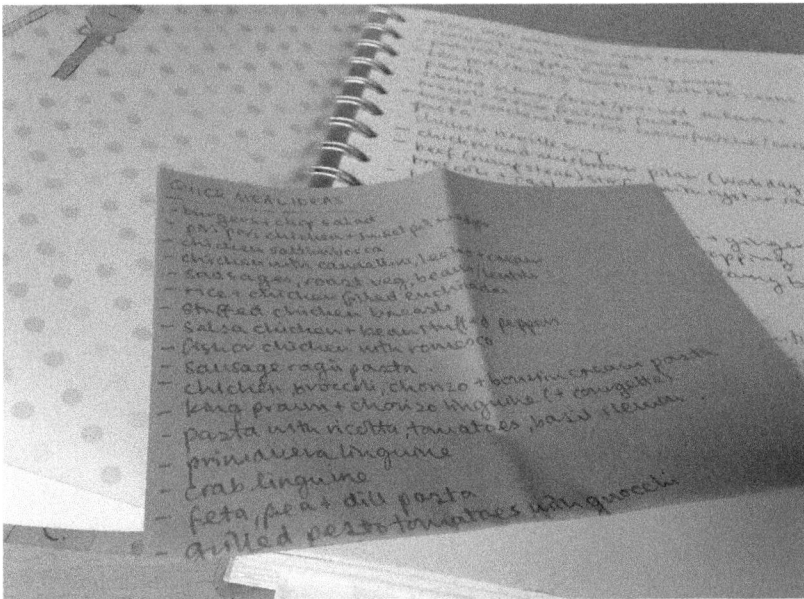

Layla notes that at the weekend 'my dad would cook something completely new, completely amazing … cooking everything from scratch, doing lots of things'. However, given the level of detail she gives to the possibilities for variety, it appears that this is something that she seeks to provide for her family through the week. In line with Parsons' findings (2016), Layla voices an additional pressure to the generation before her, which is to cook new and inspirational food on a daily basis. This is a classed activity since it concerns the display of cultural capital through diverse and varied foods. Layla's lists are particularly telling because they 'work' and are 'quick', thus indicating the temporal constraints under which she feeds the family. She also appears constantly alert to the importance of keeping a record of the meals that do work: 'then I think 'I must remember to cook that again cause everybody ate it'. Finally, as Layla suggests, her dad played a fundamental role in introducing her to new foods. This exposure has provided her with the classed skills to decipher and be attuned to recognizing the fluid boundaries of good food as a form of cultural capital, which she could build upon at university, by actively sourcing recipes. However, while her mode of feeding differs from her mother, she retains the *responsibility* for feeding. As a result, she is well practiced and efficient at the everyday managing of this cultural capital for the household, which requires constant attention and refashioning.

The second point I want to touch on is Layla's comment that her father cooked on weekends. Many participants referenced their fathers as special occasion cooks, and some female participants noted that their male partners cook on the weekend. Before taking a specific look at the household meal to illustrate how feeding operates to produce middle-class families, I first wish to consider the male participants' contribution to feeding the household.

Masculinity and feeding

There is a small, but growing, body of literature which focuses on men's everyday experiences of and approaches to cooking (Szabo 2012, 2014; Klasson and Ulver 2015; Neuman et al 2017; Warde et al 2017). Given the self-selecting nature of the sample, unsurprisingly many male participants in this study participated in cooking for the household. Nevertheless, the female participants were still much more likely to do all, or most, of the weekday cooking. This is in line with research which clearly establishes that men are more likely to have household meals prepared for them than are women (Yates and Warde 2017). Interestingly, the women in this study were not passive in taking on the everyday responsibility of feeding the household. Indeed, this emerged as an important part of their identity. On the whole, the women appeared to proactively take on this role of providing food, which as Haukanes (2007) suggests, serves to position them as 'proper' women as well as create family members as 'proper' people. Nevertheless, taking responsibility for feeding the household is an aspect of their identity that appeared difficult to shed. Mary cooked all the household meals because her partner could not cook, except for the barbeque:

KG:	When he does the barbeque, do you cook on it or do you do any ...?
Mary (35–44):	I'm not allowed anywhere near it. No, no (laughs) ...
KG:	(Laughs)
Mary:	I'll get all the stuff in the kitchen ready, get the table ready, do the drinks and just supply him with meat to cook. Like if I go over and suggest something looks like it might be about done, I'm told to mind my own business, so, yeah ... (laughs).

Mary's story portrays her as willingly casting aside her cooking skill and experience and adopting a supportive role. This is despite her acknowledgement of her superior judgement of knowing that the meat may be almost done. Nevertheless, her accompanied laughter about being told to mind her own business denotes the irony of the situation because cooking for the family *is* her business on every other occasion. In line with

Klasson and Ulver's findings (2015), Mary's partner masculinizes his cooking and detaches it from domesticity. The barbeque becomes an occasion for the dramatization of cooking, something which is ordinarily relegated to the mundane. Importantly, Mary takes on an active role in enabling his performance, albeit via a demoted role of preparing the drinks and supplying him with the meat. Finally, while Mary's experience of cooking is as an 'other-oriented responsibility', her partner appears to experience cooking as a 'self-orientated leisure' (Szabo 2014: 18). He is cooking in situations which are free from obligation and time constraints – a barbeque at the weekend.

In contrast, some male participants (and male partners of female participants) were responsible for cooking everyday, such as Irene's husband. But as the excerpt here about cooking for her adult-aged sons illustrates, heteronormative frameworks persisted, aligning an overall responsibility for feeding others with women.

Irene (55–64):	I just do it [cooking] because I have to. And I'm quite happy for [husband] to do it and he enjoys it, so er … but I think that's because I've done it all my life. He's really just taken over since he started to work part-time and I was working full-time, so he was at home and he started to do the cooking and really enjoys it.
KG:	So what is it about cooking that you don't particularly like that much?
Irene:	I think it's just because it's something you've done for so many years you lose interest don't you? (laughs) … And I do cook. I mean yesterday I cooked the bolognaise from scratch, made the las … and cooked the sauce and made the lasagnes. It doesn't … you know I do do it. But I just wouldn't list it as one of my ten favourite things to do or anything like that.
KG:	(laughs) So would [husband] make a lasagne for the boys and things like that?
Irene:	No, no.
KG:	Does he do … ?
Irene:	No he wouldn't do that one.
KG:	Right.
Irene:	He would do the bolognaise, but he wouldn't bother making the lasagne.
KG:	Right ok. Why is that?
Irene:	I think its … that's something I've always done and he doesn't like lasagne particularly. So I don't make one for us, I make it for everybody else, but not us.

Irene's quote illuminates a stark contrast between her own and her husband's experience of and approach to cooking. She has cooked all her life, she says, and it was not until her husband started working part time that he took over the responsibility. Previously, she suggests, she cooked out of obligation as opposed to her husband, who enjoys it. Nevertheless, even within this switch of domestic responsibility, the care-orientated aspect of her feeding work is still apparent. For instance, she said that just yesterday she had cooked a lasagne because her husband 'doesn't like lasagne particularly'. The lasagne she cooked was not for her and her husband, but for her mother and grown-up children who live in their own households. Hence, while Irene suggests that she does not enjoy cooking, that she willingly retains the duty for nurturing family members through the flow of food, highlights the active ways she retains her feeding role. As I will now further explore, many female participants actively and knowingly took on the main feeding work.

Active women

As is now apparent, the theme of gender is prominent in all food narratives, and it was even notable in the initial stages of this research where a specific recruitment strategy was required to secure all but three male participants. In the case of Irene for example, even though she is no longer the primary cook, she came forward for interview. It appears the 'other-oriented' female role stretches beyond the provision and preparation of food to being responsible for representing the household. But even of the men that came forward for participation, female partners sometimes stepped forward in the moment of interview, to interrupt, to correct or in some cases were called upon by my male participants to answer questions. I touched on this in Chapter 3 in my discussion of Kelly's interruption in John's description of the contents of the food cupboards. For the purposes of discussion here though, I would like to explore how the contributions of these female partners centred on the household management of food.

Gregg was primarily responsible for the everyday domestic cooking. When I arrived at our first interview, he and his partner, Becky, had just returned from the fishmongers and Becky was pre-portioning salmon to be frozen for their toddler. Becky was partially present during both interviews. In the first interview which mainly focused on attitudes and preferences, she did not interrupt implying that she was happy with the way that Gregg articulated the family's food preferences to me. In the second interview, however, when it came to showing me the intricate dynamics of how the household operated to produce food, she interrupted. This was during our conversation about expiry dates:

Gregg:	So with fruit and veg probably not, with meat yes. But typically even with meat you could … you can smell it or you can see if it's gone off, so I wouldn't be against using stuff if it was over its sell-by-date if I felt that it smelt and looked ok.
KG:	Right and do you do that then with meat?
Gregg:	Yeah.
KG:	Yeah. And would that be for everybody? For [son] as well, or just you guys?
Gregg:	No everyone yeah. As long as it … as long it's you know … if it's not massively over, like because of the way that we plan the meals …
Becky:	We don't … sorry (comes into kitchen) … we don't eat out of date meat, no.
Gregg:	No but in terms of like if … something was a day over, I'm not going to chuck it sort of thing, if it smells ok.
Becky:	Oh I don't know. I disagree.
Gregg:	Well with chicken obviously you've got to be a bit more careful but with beef and lamb …
Becky:	Doesn't tend to last that long.
Gregg:	I don't … I can't recall an example of when we've used meat recently that has been out of date.

This extended excerpt demonstrates two themes. First is that even though Gregg's participation in cooking is care-oriented in that he is responsible for cooking for the family, he nevertheless configures a masculinized identity when he talks about feeding. He draws on expertise about meat to ascertain what is edible, enabling him to position his domestic-self through knowledge. In other moments, Gregg does draw on feminized frames relating to care and nurturing about the daily feeding of his wife and son. At the same time, however, he speaks about this feeding work in masculinist terms. Earlier he had noted that his wife is responsible for the planning and shopping of food because she sticks 'rigidly' to what is needed for the week's recipes, whereas he is more likely to go 'off-piste' and buy alternative foods. The term off-piste conjures up images of Gregg's potential to explore the unknown to seek out new foods, effectively reproducing his 'foodie masculinity' (Cairns et al 2010: 607). Second, and related, is that his wife's interjection is in relation to his performance of modestly reckless masculinity around the organization and planning of food. It is assertive and has the effect of making him revise his claim that he would use out-of-date meat. Combined, their narratives reproduce Becky's domestic authority and capacities for the efficient management of feeding the household.

I have thus far suggested that while the possibility of household food work is open across gender, the everyday aspects of domestic feeding remained with the women of this sample. Men, be it participants' fathers or male partners, were rarely aligned with the household management of food. However, the women's active involvement in the provisioning of food suggests that this domestic responsibility was not passively occupied by the female participants in this research. Indeed, it could be a performance of cultural competence around ideas of reflexive involvement with caregiving through food, thus enabling participants to position take on a class and gender hierarchy. Like the personal recipe folders, it could be read as a kind of identity work in which women engage to reproduce themselves and their families culturally and socially. Given their levels of responsibility regarding feeding the household, it appeared crucial that women's food spaces, the fruits of their labour, would be seen by me, as the researcher, as displaying the right sort of cultural capital.

Furthermore, just as participants differentiated themselves from not making an effort to invest in 'good' food, the women in the sample appeared quick to distance themselves from being the sort of woman who passively takes on the domestic food work. Many female participants noted that they feed the household out of choice: because they enjoy it, or for practical reasons such as skill and having more time than their male partners. The centrality of choice to justify their roles of provisioning food are apparent in Jane and Sara's separate comments:

Sara: I do pretty much all of the food buying. Not because you know, it's a prearranged role or anything, but just I do pretty much all of the cooking, just cause I really enjoy it.

Jane (45–54):   I think once you get quite quick at doing things and you know how things cook … like my husband would take forever to cook something from scratch which he does … you know if he's cooking dinner, I'll say 'start at 2 in the afternoon, it might be ready at 6' you know (laughs). Whereas I could cook the same thing in probably a third of the time because I know what I'm doing and I'm more proficient because I've just done it for longer and I suppose I enjoy… because I enjoy it, you know I do more of it than him.

DeVault suggests that while it is important to acknowledge that food work is meaningful and rewarding for women, this work is carried out in the shadow of social and cultural expectations which position and reproduce women as responsible for the maintenance of the household and for pleasing others (1991). As Harriet notes:

'I don't mind if James ignores my food, but I just sort of feel well it's there, at least I did it. So it is quite important. It's like how … it's part of how I define my role in the house and I do see myself as the provider of the food.' (Harriet, 55–64)

Evidently, the point of Harriet's role is not whether her husband appreciates her food, but that she fulfils a role as 'a provider of food'. Her quote highlights the ways her identity is configured via ideas of caregiving through food, such that it is important to *her* that her role is fulfilled: 'well it's there, at least I did it', she says. Elsewhere, Harriet mentions that her husband was overweight:

'My husband is very overweight, (pause) but (laughs) I don't really feel responsible for that because I'm not. Does that sound really …? (pause) Like I sort of feel well … I mean I don't … I don't serve very, very fatty food deliberately. I just serve what I consider to be a fairly normal diet. If he came in and said 'right. I'm going to follow this diet so that I can lose some weight, will you help?' I probably would but he … I would get behind that, but he doesn't. He just sort of says things like 'oh I need to lose weight' and then does nothing about it.' (Harriet)

This narrative is interesting because on the one hand, Harriet is clear that she is not responsible for her husband's weight, especially since he has not been proactive about dieting. Yet on the other, her unfinished question 'does that sound really …?' and the hesitancy thereafter suggest that that maybe her husband's weight should be her responsibility and that perhaps she needs to justify her response by saying she does not deliberately serve 'very fatty food'. Her justification seems to suggest that she is uncomfortable with appearing to condone his fatness. Nevertheless, she is clear that there are limits to her levels of responsibility in catering for her husband. While her feeding work is other-orientated, this is not a passive position. In fact, the narrative is more about her husband's passivity than hers. In order for her to take on the responsibility for her husband's diet, she is quite clear that her efforts ought to be matched by him.

Previous studies have identified female participants as prioritizing their male partner's tastes (for example Charles and Kerr 1988; DeVault 1991). However, unsurprisingly since over 30 years has passed, in my research, husbands and male partners were not the focus of female participants' cooking. For instance, Layla noted that when she is planning her meals, she prioritizes her children's preferences, adding:

'My husband's [preferences] are probably low down the list (laughs). He tends to like what I make. He only doesn't like it if I give him a dish that doesn't have meat in basically, and then he pokes around in it and looks for the chicken and I tell him no actually, it's just got butternut squash in it.' (Layla)

Notably, while her husband is 'low down the list', Layla's own tastes are not mentioned at all. Like many female participants responsible for feeding children, her primary focus is ensuring that their children are fed a diverse range of healthy foods. However, as much as this is about pleasing others it is also about a gendered responsibility for the classed intergenerational reproduction of capital as we will now explore.

Fashioning a taste for diversity

Bourdieu (1996) notes that the family is a primary site for the accumulation and transmission of capital. He also argues that: 'each field calls forth and gives life to a specific form of interest, a specific *illusion*, as tacit recognition of the value of the stakes of the game and as practical mastery of its rules' (Bourdieu and Wacquant 1992: 117; italics original). To recap, interest is defined by one's position in the game and the journey which brings each player to that position in the game. As such, the 'mastery' of taste requires recognition of its value, which, once recognized, enables its conversion into capital, depending on a player's position in the field. I will now consider how participants with children passed down a disposition to recognize certain foods as being indicative of good taste to equip their children with inherited capital. Beagan et al note that parents (usually mothers) prioritize inculcating certain tastes in their children, arguing that feeding the family is about the 'transmission of tastes, dispositions, and logics of practice through which people perform their identities and distinguish themselves from others in social hierarchies' (2015: 239). Interestingly in my analysis, this intergenerational reproduction was always spoken about in relation to broader public narratives about junk food, obesity and the importance of variation for example. Thus, while the hierarchy within the field remains, its associated specific form of interest must be understood in relation to the broader narratives which influence and reproduce social rules. In light of this, I direct analysis towards the ways in which my participants strove to transmit an understanding of these social rules around taste to their children. In line with findings so far, fashioning a taste for diversity and being open to foods emerged as substantial and important for the intergenerational reproduction of cultural capital in participant households. As one parent noted, exposing children to diversity is worthy of constant perseverance: 'I just think you keep plugging away at that and eventually they'll like it'.

All parents talked at length about introducing their children to new foods and displayed pride around their children being open to new foods. As the following three separate quotes illustrate, pride operates around the success at ensuring that their children display a disposition for good food:

Carla (45–54):	And I would never buy meat from McDonalds. Ever.
KG:	Why is that?
Carla:	Because I think it's junk.
KG:	Do you take … have the kids been to McDonalds?
Carla:	My eldest's been twice, after his gym competitions because that's his … what he would like as his reward (laughs), (pause) … you know I haven't taken the others, but they've probably been … they've probably been occasionally, you know with a friend or sometimes at parties people order in chicken nuggets or something don't they? I mean I don't know … it's not a regular thing anyway. They're probably pretty militant about food. They all … they all get that we need to eat nice food (laughs).
Ed (65+):	My son went on work experience when he was 15 with the school … all the other kids were having burgers, chips and fish and things, and he said 'Now can I have the duckling a l'orange please?' (laughs) and went back up for second helpings you know.
Mary:	Even when he was a baby, like I was always trying really hard to try and give him lots of like different things to eat and make sure he wasn't going to be one of these dead fussy kids. And he's not too … like then they get fussier as they get older don't they? But he's not too bad, like he'll try most things so I'm quite fortunate in that … you know, if … like on Friday night, [husband] was away so me and [son] just went out for dinner and he wanted Thai (laughed). So we went for Thai food (laughed) on Friday, which is really nice, cause I know like quite often your choices with your kids it's like burger or pizza or something, but he's quite sort of open to lots of different things.

Disgust and distinction are working here in tandem. Participants' boundary-marking around their children's propensity to appreciate either healthy or exotic foods is clearly articulated in relation to their understanding of bad food. The symbolic value in Thai food or duckling a l'orange for example lies not in the food itself, but in its relationality to banal and 'unhealthy foods', which surface in participant narratives time and time again. For these participants, it appears necessary to position 'nice food' alongside 'junk' to display their children's good food habits and demonstrate their capacities as parents to produce children who make the right choices, even when children around them are choosing burgers, chicken nuggets, pizzas and chips. Oncini (2020) finds that parental social training around food fosters a social recognition that a disposition for omnivorousness and health signals distinction and enables the construction of boundaries from a very early age. These participant excerpts echo this finding and their commitment it seems has paid off, such that their children are 'militant about food' and 'open to lots of different things' – except, of course, being open to the pizzas or burgers that could not carry the same distinction. Again these narratives, framed in terms of making choices, are limited to foods which are situated as distant from uncultivated palates. In addition, being committed to producing children who are open-tasters as opposed to fussy-eaters has the effect of positioning the participants as committed, even sophisticated, parents.

In what follows, Julie talks at length about the importance of providing her two boys a wide variety of foods:

Julie (35–44):	Once they get to a certain age, 'that's your tea, and get on with it, or go without'. So, we've never lost (laughs). We've had to compromise many times, but we've never lost that battle.
KG:	And is that important to you?
Julie:	Yeah. We did fajitas and Harry's fine with fajitas, he'll eat the pepper and the onion, Keiran just wouldn't. We'd rolled it up because we thought if we hide it, but he just wouldn't eat it. So the compromise was: we made him a fresh one up with just a bit of chicken in. And he ate it, you know. You've got to be aware that there are certain food tastes that they just will not like. Harry tried a bit of butternut squash when we made this Spanish stew up and they ate the chicken and the chorizo from it, and we gave them a piece of butternut squash each. Harry said he would try it. He tried it and spat it out and started crying (laughs). So you know, that's obviously, he really didn't like it.

Like parents in Gram and Grøhhøj's study (2015), Julie's children are expected to taste the food served. She is clear that she understands their individual tastes yet overrides their preference. Julie and her husband have never lost that battle, although they have had to compromise. But the compromises she makes are downplayed. After giving her son a fajita, she notes 'the compromise was: we made him a fresh one up with just a bit of chicken in'. In fact, she made her son an entirely new chicken wrap, after he had rejected the initial one in which she had hidden onion and pepper. Nevertheless, rather than suggesting that she accommodated her son's narrow tastes, she presents a narrative that he will either eat what she expects him to eat or that he is at least open to being exposed to new foods. Julie seems to maintain a position of authority through the performance of a kind of feeding work which is orientated towards producing autonomous and independent children, who are open to trying new foods. However, she makes discerning judgements around which foods are worthy of perseverance. Interestingly, contrary to situating her children as open-tasters, this has the effect of limiting their autonomy, thus reproducing her own childhood experiences of lacking choice.

Narratives about perseverance in exposing children to good foods, highlight that good taste is not innate, but rather a strategic inclination to persevere to be open to or to appreciate certain foods is a result of cultural capital. While couched within frames of diversity, Julie implements controls around food to encourage tastes for health and diversity. In doing so, she transmits cultural capital to her children via feeding, which they can take out of the home and draw on as future middle-class adults. Julie goes on to emphasize that this requires effort:

> 'You want them to have choices, they're growing up as well. They need to have a bit of choice, but ... I don't know it is hard. It's a hard one and I think that's why often we'll eat separately from them. But it's ... trying things at school. In a maths lesson they'd had some Dorito crisps Harry was saying he'd tried some Reggae Reggae Sauce, and he said he really liked it. So if they come back with anything positive that they've tried this and they liked this, I'll go and buy it or try and find it. And it's trying ... sometimes we'll dumb down what we eat. So try and find a balance in the middle. Try and lift them up a little bit from their comfort zone but we'll pull ourselves down a bit so we can try and eat something a bit similar.' (Julie)

Julie suggests that she would seek out new foods, in response her son's experience of trying Reggae Reggae Sauce. However, there is an implication here that had he voiced the same positivity about Dorito crisps, she would not make similar efforts. Doritos are something he 'had' as opposed to 'tried', and crisps cannot be appraised via frames of health, authenticity or exoticness. Furthermore, Julie notes that when they eat together as a family, she attempts to strike a balance between everyone's differing tastes. Her comment that 'we'll dumb down what we eat' to 'lift them up' both reproduces a taste hierarchy as well as signposts towards the negotiations and compromises she makes in relation to fashioning a taste for diversity in her children at the household meal.

Many participants noted that eating together was an important means to establish a disposition for their children to learn appropriate tastes, which for the most part centred on being open to particular foods. Several participants said that their food habits did not change with the arrival of children, since they were motivated to have their children join them at the household table at an early age. For instance:

> 'But it wasn't long before she was eating the same as us, just obviously pureed and all the rest of it. So I don't really remember and we didn't … we didn't eat all that differently. I didn't pander to her being a baby particularly. I think we may have … it's slightly, slightly plainer food perhaps, but (pause) I can't remember. Actually I can't remember but I don't remember it being much of an interruption, put it that way.' (Harriet)

While comments such as this are framed in terms of children fitting in with the household, there is nevertheless a 'heightened child-centeredness' (Ochs and Kremer-Sadlik 2015: 89) implicit in these narratives. As Harriet suggests they ate 'slightly plainer foods' and as Julie suggests, they 'dumb down' their tastes. The care work involved in balancing child and adult food tastes requires dedication and negotiation. As the following section will illustrate, this care work extends to the organization of time to ensure the staging of the household meal.

Sharing time, sharing food: ideal family meals

This concluding section looks towards the family meal – sometimes achieved, sometimes not. Read as the final moment of domestication, it is a practice where households come together symbolically and physically to enact good food through familial bonding. Regardless of participants' individualized notions of good food, this final moment of household good food was scaffolded by gendered and classed food work. Thus, I argue that little has changed since Charles and Kerr's (1988) oft-quoted study in which participants defined a 'proper meal' as a social occasion entailing family members coming together at a table to share food, which is cooked by a woman. Given the multiple strands required to facilitate this occasion, the staging of the family meal requires prioritization and time.

The frequency that households eat together at a table varied across the sample, but all participants indicated eating together is a preferred practice and all participants with children noted that their children ate at the table. Those participants who said that they eat in front of the television did so with justifications, acknowledging the norm of eating at the table. For instance: "I would love to say that we sit down at the kitchen table every time, but I'd say, no – weeknights it tends to be here on the sofa and then the occasional meal at the table" (Ian).

Other participants noted that eating in front of the television is 'naughty' or 'not great' in confessional tones, and a repeated pattern across the sample was that phones and tablet devices have no place at the family meal. This implies an overall recognition that social bonding processes are key to the family meal and that by shifting the focus away from conversation, these technologies remove the potential to perform a particular version of family over the convivial sharing of food. In short, technology is positioned in a similar way to convenience foods: in direct opposition to doing family through food.

I now return to primarily focus on households with children, since in this research the family meal emerged as an important means to deliver children with a carefully monitored range of foods and provide them with a repertoire from which to make responsible choices. Juliette's quote here describes an occasion when her and her husband eat separately from their children:

KG: When it's just the two of you here and you say have a curry takeaway or when you're just eating, the two of you, what happens then? Is it different to when the children are with you?

Juliette: Well sadly because the curry is usually on a Friday night, I'm afraid we'll usually have it while watching the telly and hoping there's a Bruce Willis film on or something (laughs). It's kind of part of a whole cultural experience like, 'yes, I'm having a take away so I haven't cooked this dinner and I'm watching a blockbuster' (laughs) … yeah so it is different because with the children, *very* occasionally, as a treat, they'll be allowed to eat in front of the telly. But by and large we eat at the table. But if they're not watching then sometimes we eat in front of the television (said in a whisper)

Juliette says her children *very* occasionally eat in front of the television and situates the table as pivotal to the family meal. She clearly marks herself (and her family) apart from the type of person who eats in front of the television. But for her and her husband, having a takeaway curry on a Friday night marks a domestic moment which is free from the emotional and physical labour of staging the family meal. The explicit connection she makes is between eating a takeaway and watching a Bruce Willis film. She suggests that if she is going to let herself slip and indulge in takeaway food, then watching television, and specifically enjoying the facile offerings of a Hollywood movie, is acceptable. There is an implicit suggestion that the inferiority of these two cultural forms go hand-in-hand; they are convenient, and their consumption requires little effort. Distinction, nonetheless, can be attached to their consumption through the provision of irony around watching a blockbuster being a 'cultural experience'.

Central to Juliette's narrative is that eating dinner in front of the television is not normal practice, despite my original question being about what she and her husband are doing when they eat separately from the children. She appears to have a heightened awareness of the importance of presenting a household to me who eats at the dinner table and that eating a takeaway in front of the television (from the lack of preparation of the food to the lack of conversation, and without the prop of the table) is not the norm and requires justification. Furthermore, she concludes her response in a whispered tone that this is done without her children watching. That is, not only is it a guilty pleasure, but also it is important to her that her children's food experiences, observed and practiced, are centred around convivial eating at the table. Participant narratives tended to situate the family meal as a significant bonding practice which acted to expand children's tastes, instil a capacity to engage with variety, and provide children with the skills to recognize good food and discern which foods are worthy of critical evaluation. Considering that participants on the whole drew on notions of choice and abundance in relation to food preferences and practices, passing on this capacity to make active, discerning choices was a key concern for the parents of the sample. But again, it centred on restriction as much as choice.

That the occasion of the family meal was prioritized by participants reflects classed ideologies around the performance of the family through food. In all households the valuing of the family meal was often spoken about in relation to public narratives about its perceived decline. Take Philip for example: "I think nowadays it's a little more dispersed isn't it? That families perhaps don't do that as much, but certainly when we were growing up we did. It wouldn't have been acceptable"(Philip, 55–64).

Even if not always achieved, all participants living with other household members displayed a commitment to gathering the household around the table to share a meal which is contrary to political and even academic claims (for instance, Daniels 2012; Skeer and Ballard 2013) that the family meal is in decline. Like Philip's comment, there is a suggestion that the family meal is a practice almost defunct and that this is a result of a dispersion of family networks. Yates and Warde argue that the ideological dominance of the family meal is evidence of 'the continuing joint strength of custom, preference and necessity' (2017: 114). In line with this, participants seemed to display a heightened awareness of an idealized image of the family meal as being a necessary means of enacting family. Moreover, that participants established and prioritized the family meal to synchronize the multiple time-space paths of the household, is evidence of its ideological value. As Neil suggests:

'It binds us together as a family. Particularly with us all … as the kids have got older, spinning off and sitting in front of screens and electronics the whole time. I mean we don't even watch telly together. It's very rare that we even do that, so it's the thing that binds us together.' (Neil, 45–54)

Neil positions the pulls of technology as a threat to family time, and maintains that sharing food acts, to use Wilks' words, 'as a kind of universal family glue' (2010: 429). It is a domestic occasion worthy of protecting because it brings the family together when the household, especially the children, is 'spinning off' in different directions. Des also hints that households are more fragmented:

'I think society is more atomized than it was and it does take an effort to eat together and I think we make a you know … if you lose the habit I think it sometimes difficult to get that. We don't eat food in front of the … I mean we sometimes eat in front of the TV but it's not … it's not a regular thing.' (Des)

Like Neil, Des posits that eating together is difficult to achieve because society is more 'atomized'. Like Juliette, his narrative situates the television in opposition to the family meal, and he distances himself from this mode of eating. Importantly, Des suggests that it takes *effort* to eat together, suggesting that this occasion is difficult to achieve but worthy of prioritizing. That participants actively prioritize this mode of eating suggests that this is an occasion worthy of investment. By sharing time and space, the bonding processes established during the family meal are an important vehicle for passing on cultural capital through food.

Across the sample, participants noted that the family meal was important for familial bonding. My point here is not to question the extent to which households are fragmented or not, but to highlight how perceptions of fragmented timespaces and external interruptions (such as technology) are operating behind participant understandings of coming together and sharing food. Daly (2001) argues that when family time is labelled as scarce, it becomes increasingly idealized. Families reaffirming togetherness over food is meaningful when read against ideas that households are 'atomized', 'dispersed' and 'spinning off' in different directions. It is an occasion worthy of protection from the changing dynamics of family time. Implicit in the idea that the family meal is hard to accomplish, is the notion that achieving it requires that participants make 'an effort', as Des suggests. Importantly, the effort required to prioritize the family extends beyond sourcing and preparing food to include the coordination of family time and space within a multitude of constraints. Moreover, eating together is valued when it is achieved away from external cultural flows (such as the television), such that the final moment of domesticating food can be read as reaffirming values of intimate familial living. Understood in this light, participants' prioritization of eating together reflects the importance of the family meal as a moment to reaffirm family values. The ideal of the family meal held such strong currency across all interviews, denoting participants' cultural and social orientation towards the practice (achieved or not) of sharing food as a means to establish and reinforce familial bonds. These bonding processes are pivotal in reproducing symbolic value in certain foods and relatedly the production of middle-class identities.

Conclusion

In this chapter, I have scrutinized the early childhood learning processes providing the initial structures of early food experiences forming the basis of the habitus. Revisiting participants' life journeys, I have explored their ways of knowing about food in relation to narratives about the importance of abundance, choice and diversity. Exploring this trajectory has allowed for a nuanced understanding of the ways that participants' logic of practice is comprised of (feminized) generative learning supplemented with accrued culinary capital, as the discussion about cookbooks suggests. Cookbooks enable the enactment of the (selective) diversity associated with good food, and at the same time, cookbooks can act as anchors to personal history. Moreover, personal recipe folders reveal gendered generational bonds between the female participants and other female family members. While the majority of the cohort distanced themselves from their childhood tastes, they nevertheless reproduced a disposition to invest in food as a form of cultural capital.

The family meal emerged as a priority in this research as a means to enact family through talk over food. Participants appeared reflexive about the work involved in its production, not least in the scheduling of time it requires but also the work, or effort, involved in attaching symbolic value to food. It appears worth it though because the family meal is an occasion to bond and enact intimate relationships over particular types of food. For the parents in the sample, the family meal is an occasion to deliver food-related social training. This training is integral to the intergenerational reproduction of capital through the teaching of making appropriate food choices, which reflect and reproduce classed understandings of good taste. The family meal acts as an important household event to instil a naturalized logic of practice in children to be (selectively) open to diversity, and in so doing, implicitly builds middle-class future-consumers. The family meal is also a key moment to reiterate gendered values around practice. In most households, the staging of this event was the result feminized feeding work involving the domestication of carefully selected external processes, which are then symbolically and physically integrated into the family via food. These processes, which I have shown extend well beyond the home, culminate in the display of a family habitus which is orientated to make careful, considered food selections from the global marketplace.

In the context of our research interactions, through food, participants were able to show the values which produce themselves, their family, and their household. Such values centre on making an effort, active choosing, investing in health and diversity, and the mediation of particular knowledge sources to ensure good food is delivered to the table. Much like their understandings of choice and taste, participants drew on social understandings of the ordered practice of sharing food at a table. These are inherently classed understandings and demonstrated through differentiation to an imagined mass. On the one hand, participants articulated notional individualism through their tastes and preferences. On the other hand, they understood and enacted the domestic sharing of food in relation to a social world in which the family meal is ideologically positioned as a way to achieve intimate togetherness in fragmented times. From staging the family meal, to sourcing ingredients and information, the sample collectively mobilized shared culinary knowledge implying a shared recognition of a general and classed orientation to invest in particular foods and modes of provisioning as having value.

As the concluding chapter will argue, participant performances of good food in the domestic sphere relates to the reproduction of class privilege. Given the classed positioning of my participants, I will argue that participant prioritization of particular foods and ways of eating, denotes a recognition of the importance of 'playing the game' successfully, a capacity for which requires exchangeable dominant capital. This in turn suggests that Bourdieu's model of accumulation based on knowledge and perception of future value is applicable for this sample. Through their possession of legitimate capital, participants were able to attach value to their food practices to convert, accrue and generate value for themselves (Skeggs 2011). In other words, this recognition of the ways in which individuals can be implicated through their food choices and the importance of having good taste, serves as a resource to be exchanged within the field for privilege.

6

Conclusion

The interpretations which form the basis of this book are based on rigorous analysis of visual and verbal data co-produced in domestic settings. Of course, had someone else with contrasting experiences and perspectives interpreted the data, a different story could have emerged. But social research cannot claim to uncover a single objective and universal truth; there is always more than one version of the story.

The story this book tells is about the intimate ways that class is connected, through food, to identity and the home. I have recounted data which starts from participants' childhoods and traced their journeys into the established households in which our research conversations took place. From this vantage point, I learnt about the ways in which respondents incorporate food and ideas about food into their homes to arrive at the point of eating. I have looked towards everyday practices of domestic food provisioning with the aim of understanding how in middle-class settings some foods and modes of eating are valued and normalized, while others are implicitly and explicitly rejected and othered. This sample of 27 self-selected participants residing in the North East of England is by no means representative of the British 'middle classes'. However, I contend that these small-scale domestic interactions have implications for a broader understanding of the relational ways that class both provides access to particular ways of eating and reproduces eaters who participate in very specific ways of valuing 'good' food. In this final chapter, I gather together the themes which have emerged in this book to offer a concluding discussion about the broader implications of taste, middle-class identities, and domestic food provisioning in contemporary Britain.

Reflexive identities

Ingrid: I apologize that The Archers has just come on (laughs). It sounds so middle class (laughs).

KG: I remember now you said you listened to the Archers while you had your tea (laughs)

Participants were recruited for this research based on my assumptions that they were located in middle-class social positions. Interview talk highlighted the contested ways that participants related to their class position. Reflecting research which highlights the ambiguity of class belongingness (Savage 2000; Friedman et al 2021), overall participants struggled against social categorization, specifically as being seen as middle class in any straightforward way. Participants could have been pushing back against some of my framing assumptions by insisting *against* their evident middle-classness. But in the context of our research encounters, it appeared rather that by elaborating the complexity of their self-understandings and biographies, participants were aiming to present themselves as unique and distant from *any* form of classification or collective belonging. This speaks powerfully to postmodern debates about reflexive individualism. What is particularly striking in this regard is that participants understood that there is value in reflexive individuality, both in their talk about class and in their food tastes. As Ingrid's quote suggests, this value lies in the recognition of what class practices might look like, which through humour can almost be situated as separate from a more enduring, complex, and authentic self. And yet, humour is not neutral. Used by Ingrid as a tool for deflection, it provides insight into the complexities entailed in differentiation: in this case to being middle class. In this sense, class becomes an identity category which can be reflexively appropriated – and therefore reflexively refused or denied. As a result, identity is situated as the property of an individual rather than a collective category. The point I want to make here is that these participants appeared relatively comfortable in marking themselves as too biographically and culturally complex to be reduced to a class category. While this has the effect of displacing class, it simultaneously remakes and reproduces middle-classness. Paying attention to practice highlighted that my participants' recognition of the value of individuality was collectively shared across the sample. Furthermore, this entailed the drawing of distinctions in relation to ideas of the mass.

Valued displays of reflexive individuality are classed because they require cultural and economic capital. This cohort resided in middle-class positions. It follows, then, that they have the dominant capital to reflexively appropriate certain kinds of identity. If the field marks a social space wherein people can accrue and exchange capital for valued identities, then valued identities can only be available to those who have the capitals to enter the field in the first place. As Skeggs (2011) reminds us, those outside the field are valueless on account of their social position of exclusion. They can only ever be defined through their lack. It is in this way that Bourdieu's concept of habitus (the embodiment of capitals inherited and strategically accrued over time) is of direct relevance to this study. Habitus provides a way to understand how *valued* subjects are made (Skeggs 2011, 2004a). Common to participant food narratives is that they centred on valuing self-investment through prioritizing the acquisition and provision of 'good' food. But this was not always narrated in a straightforward way. While eating and feeding household members with certain types of food emerged as important to these participants, *not* eating certain foods emerged as a much more significant. Participant modes of self-investment through food appeared to be more about rejecting an imagined figure of a mass consumer, which is implicitly marked as working class.

Identities are of course relational, and the findings of this research support Bourdieu's (1984) now well-known claims that the middle classes perform distinction through distinguishing themselves from a working-classed mass. But this analysis shows too that some of the value of the middle-class performance of individuality lies in its reflexive nature. For instance, when participants 'confessed' to their 'occasional' use of convenience foods or eating in front of the television, they performed a critical awareness about the lack of value in these foods and ways of eating, which acted to authorize their more authentic food identities. As in Ingrid's statement, some participants demonstrated ironic knowingness around coding practices and tastes as middle class or not. Participants then displayed heightened critical reflexivity of themselves and the foods they eat. This matters because it is a way of working to mark themselves apart from an uncritical mass. Marking the self as different from the mass requires that the mass be invalidated. It also involves the assumption that the mass is knowable, homogeneous, even simple, implicitly marked as unreflexively consuming the wrong sorts of food.

Against this reductive figure of the unreflexive mass consumer, the middle-class participants in this study separately – but in exactly the same ways – emphasized their own difference and reflexivity. They presented themselves as prioritizing homemade food, critically selecting foods from the marketplace, and talked about their household's eating habits in frames of diversity. Class consciousness seemed to be operating through not belonging, even to the category of middle class. That is, the participants can be *collectively* positioned through their consensual recognition of the value in *individual* performances of reflexive diversity. Consistent within this idea is that the construction of valued personhood requires dominant capital for self-investment as 'tacit recognition of the value of the stakes of the game and as practical mastery of its rules' (Bourdieu and Wacquant 1992: 117). I now turn to reconsider participant life histories to show how class processes are made and drawn upon through critical selection and restriction.

Personal food histories

'Sometimes food can be used as a way to find out what class you are. And I think people ... I've been in people's houses where ... where there's almost been a probing sense where it's almost like a test, like a dance ... in my past, in going to a private school and all the rest of it, as the person on ... who's you know not paying fees for example then ... then there have been situations where food has been used to embarrass or to upset or to find out what he's made of and you quickly learn what's going on and it's an uncomfortable place to be.' (Gregg)

The life stories generated in this research capture nuanced relationships between capital accrual and life stage. Central to all participants' narratives was a sense of moving from restriction and lack of choice to abundance and diversity. Participants drew on notions of expanding choice offered by the global marketplace, suggesting that they understood their broadening of taste to be the result of a 'generational effect' (Warde 1997: 72). However, *all* participants narrated a journey of moving from lack of choice to abundance. The notion of choice appeared as a necessary frame through which participants made sense of themselves as consumers of diversity. In part, this supports Warde's (1997) findings that changes in food practices relate to life stages. But by factoring class into the analysis, it is remarkably evident that participants' transition from being fed as children to feeding themselves independently coincided with classed moments in their life trajectories. This significant insight provides a starting point from which to consider how class is implicated in participant food biographies. What these food stories tell us is that the expansion of taste is to do with individual life trajectories as well as perceptions of broader social change. These stories indicate how the accrual of capital (for instance via university) goes hand-in-hand with the capacity to display an (authorized) disposition of openness to diversity, and thereby assert and reproduce middle-class taste.

Life stories were also an important means of capturing the complexities of social mobility by highlighting moments when the habitus was ill-fitting with its position in the field of food consumption. Participants who were from established middle-class backgrounds did not display self-conscious reflexivity around personal food moments. Conversely, as Gregg's quote suggests, stories of upward mobility were punctured with 'moments of hysteresis' (Friedman 2015: 131) around food. Here, participants recognized classed aspects of these occasions yet perceived that they lacked the capital to enact legitimate food performances. This resulted in feelings of exclusion and lack. Gregg's attendance at boarding school was enabled by a full scholarship. His narrative dwelt, as in the comments just reported, on how such food moments are 'an uncomfortable place to be'. But he also suggests how 'you quickly learn what's going on', that is, to recognize the aesthetic display around food as a class 'dance'. There is a small but growing body of literature which provides qualitative accounts of social mobility (Lawler 1999; Friedman 2012; Mallman 2017, 2018), and much of this takes higher education and/or employment as its focus (for instance, Reay et al 2009;

Reay 2013, 2018; Lehmann 2014; Friedman et al 2017; Bradley 2018). To date, there is no research which pays attention to these moments of disjuncture through the lens of food. And yet, accounting for such moments is a vital way of understanding class processes. While increasingly class is understood as fragmented and individualized, the food life histories of the upwardly mobile draw attention to the boundaries of class and in particular the experience of crossing those boundaries. These '*tension points*' (Mallman 2017: 29; italics original) highlight the fraught nature of upward mobility whereby access to resources brings more possibilities, even if such possibilities are experienced with heightened reflexivity.

Studies have established that individuals experiencing social mobility relate to aspects of their working-class histories in complicated ways (Lawler 1999; Reay, Crozier and Clayton 2009; Friedman 2012, 2015; Reay 2017). The narratives of the upwardly mobile people I worked with were consistent with these insights. But regardless of shifting class positions, what is significant about my findings is that *most* participants expressed a dissonance between childhood tastes and adult tastes. Their narratives emphasized how during their life course their tastes had expanded to include a more diverse range of foods. Unsurprisingly then, there was a marked absence of foods reminiscent of childhood in participants' food cupboards. Social distance is central to the formation of taste (Bourdieu 1984). What is particularly noteworthy about these findings is what they reveal about the multi-directional flow of distance. As well as narratives which distance the self from being a (working-class) mass-consuming other, participants distanced themselves from a childhood self which is best fixed in the past. This complicates Bourdieu's idea that taste in food 'reveals the deepest dispositions of the habitus' (Bourdieu 1984: 190), because it is not as simple as tastes staying the same or changing. I discuss omnivorousness next, but in the context of thinking about food, culture and social mobility my participants were perhaps less cultural omnivores than they were 'culturally homeless' (Friedman 2012). That is, much like the upwardly mobile display ambiguity towards their childhood tastes, all participants displayed a tension between distancing themselves from their childhood tastes and shaking off learnt dispositions. These learnt dispositions were not entirely 'sedimented' in their habitus, because habitus is not rigidly set at birth. Life stories, then, suggest that taste is the outcome of personal and social history. Participants' focus on mobility not only highlights how childhood learning processes are disrupted when working-class individuals move into middle-class positions, but also that the childhood food tastes established for those born into middle-class positions are insufficient features of a middle-class habitus. While individual class starting points presuppose the possibility of acquiring further capital, for this particular sample, the possibility to enact good food centred on accrued, rather than inherited, capital to facilitate the active and reflexive reconstitution of childhood learning laid down by their parents.

The inherited tastes that participants carried with them into adulthood are deemed insufficient, then. But a repeated theme is that participants, now in middle-class positions, displayed a strategic disposition to actively invest in and display forms of culinary capital, such as cookbooks. These investments have exchange-value in a social world which prizes the importance of diverse cultural consumption. But while participants distanced themselves from passively reproducing their learnt dispositions, they also refrained from articulating a wholesale rejection of them. They often fondly shared memories and showed me passed-down culinary objects, such as crockery and cookbooks, valued for their representations of family connections to well-established culinary knowledge. But importantly, according to the valuing of plurality, these past markers of taste could be presented as having classed value through their juxtaposition with more contemporary culinary objects. Thus, distinction can be performed through an active and mediating relationship to the culinary capital available, which has the effect of producing a performance premised on individuality. Yet, across these individualized biographies and narratives, there are clear and repeated patterns. The types of culinary capital in the form of knowledge and objects that participants valued from childhood all related to the doing of homemade. Yet, many of these were commodified versions of doing homemade, in the same way as the types of contemporary culinary capital they acquired. The recurrence of Jamie Oliver, Yotam Ottolenghi, Nigel Slater and Nigella Lawson across the sample's cookbook collections alongside culinary items which centre on romanticizing thrift and tradition, for example, was remarkable. This shared (mis)recognition of the social valuing of nostalgia alongside up-to-date food modes indicates how this cohort could exchange a variation of cultural forms for value. It is in these relations of exchange that the specific diets of the participants and their households are reproduced as valued. This has important implications for middle-class reproduction as I will now go on to show.

Intergenerational reproduction of culinary capital

'My daughter's first proper solid savoury food was mashed up chicken korma with rice (laughs). I was so proud (laughs).' (Juliette)

Analysis established that households prioritize the intergenerational reproduction of cultural capital through food. All participants with children drew on frames of diversity in their narratives of feeding children and encouraging diverse, healthy eating habits was clearly understood as worthy of parental perseverance. Being 'open' in the late modern world is valued

(Bennett et al 2009), and this was certainly reproduced in the narratives of the parents of this sample. Cultural competence around food tastes is an important disposition to lay down in childhood teaching and learning. But as I argue in the preceding chapters, openness is selective and therefore it is in fact around taste judgement that valued dispositions are laid down. These dispositions are mostly established during the family meal which emerged as highly valued in this research, despite political and media narratives which suggest otherwise. In the intimate space of the family home, and through sharing food at the kitchen table, children are taught the social importance of diversity and the importance of being open to trying new foods. But operating within frames of openness and diversity is a clear limiting of choices, specifically around those foods which are regarded as insufficient for the appraisal of good taste. As Juliette's quote demonstrates, parents were spontaneously proud when their children ate 'exotic' and 'ethnic' foods. By contrast, when their children ate 'plain' foods these seemed to be justified and explained. This social training around taste is enacted at an everyday level and centres on selective exposure to diversity. Children are taught not to eat everything, but to make legitimized preferences. These processes are classed. They implicitly encourage an intergenerational reproduction of an orientation towards aestheticizing and valorizing a wide and varied diet as a vehicle for the display of knowledge and critical reflexivity, particularly around the notion of making healthy choices.

Warde notes that 'it seems now equally, or perhaps more, important that parents convey to their children skills and competences for the handling of new forms of culture' (2017: 152). This is particularly interesting when read in relation to the ways my participants related to their own childhood tastes. While there is a disconnection between participant's ambivalence towards the foods of their childhoods and the inculcation of taste among their own children, taste itself remains worthy of perseverance. Given that, as we have seen, the socio-historical value of food taste is always changing, the transmission of capital must be via frames of critical appraisal and nurturing (legitimate) individual preferences. That is, part of this social training around food seemed to be about arming children with the skills to negotiate the ever-changing boundaries of 'good' taste. Teaching and learning how and what foods to consume (and limit) is worthy of perseverance, because an aesthetic preference to critically discern food can be transferred to other cultural forms. This has fundamental implications for classed relations because even though ideas about what constitutes good taste shift, the transmission of cultural capital ensures that the doctrine of good taste remains intact through its recognition. Therefore, it remains the property of those with the classed resources to ensure its reproduction and reinvention. The following discussion about omnivorousness will elaborate how the display of taste involves a playoff between choice and restriction, openness and closure, in order to fashion preferences which reflect a valued aspect of middle-class habitus which encourages individualism.

Omnivorousness: critical selection

'There's not a lot that I couldn't eat now. But, I used to detest coriander, it used to make me feel ill and [husband] loves it and we found a recipe in one of the books for this Thai noodle, with … it's got prawns and crab and stuff in and it sounded lovely, but you needed to use loads of coriander and he was going on and on (laughs), 'we'll just do it, but just put a little bit', so was like 'oh this is alright' cause there was so many other strong flavours and then we just kept making it and we just upped and upped the level of coriander and now I can have coriander … you know, I can eat it in the handful. And, I really, really hated it … I'm firm believer that if I can do that, then you can sort of almost (pause) get your taste around anything. You know a lot of food tastes, anxiety issues are … you know can be changed … yeah, it's just you know you feel like you're missing out on certain things by not eating certain foods, to try and like them. And because it's worked, you know, I like … up until even when I started eating meat again, I would only eat certain meats. I wouldn't eat beef, and I certainly wouldn't have eaten a steak. Whereas now I love a steak and the bloodier the better.' (Julie)

Omnivore refers to 'a person who eats foods of all kinds' (*Oxford English Dictionary* 2023). As I explained in Chapter 2, the sociology of consumption in recent years has appropriated the term 'omnivorousness' to categorize contemporary shifts towards a preference to consume multiple cultural forms which span traditional hierarchies of high and low culture (Peterson 1992). To this, class analysis has added that social groups who possess high volumes of cultural and economic capital are more likely to display diverse cultural tastes. In addition, openness to variety and breadth of cultural consumption acts as a form of distinction: 'the required orientation is towards reflexive appropriation, in a spirit of openness, of a diversity of cultural products, but this continues to produce subtle boundaries beyond which it is not respectable to trespass' (Bennett et al 2009: 194). One of the effects of using omnivorousness in relation to cultural consumption more generally has been its dislocation from food (bar a handful of studies which by and large concentrate on 'foodies' or eating out, for instance, Cairns et al 2010; Johnston and Baumann 2014; Oleschuk 2017; Yalvaç and Hazir 2021). Here I have returned omnivorousness to the everydayness of food in relation to a group of people who are driven to being open to engaging with a diverse range of foods in the home. In so doing, I flag up the contested ways that diverse diets are experienced and preferred. The term omnivore suggests that we have a choice; the omnivore can choose to eat anything. But what became clear as the research unfolded is that while participants performed a disposition to consume diversity, this was in highly restricted ways. Participants were not open to all foods.

People's experience and understanding of diversity has often been overlooked in research into omnivorousness which foregrounds quantitatively analysing modes of consumption (Yalvaç and Hazir 2021). Drawing on life history data to explore how a disposition to consume diversity is understood by participants in relation to broader social changes helps reveal a more nuanced picture of participants' 'ways of preferring' (Daenekindt and Roose 2017). As I discussed earlier, what clearly emerges from these stories is the explicit marking of some foods as worthless. So, while Julie claims in the quote that 'there's not a lot that I couldn't eat now', elsewhere in her narrative she is clear in naming foods that she would not eat. These are ready meals, jarred sauces, processed foods, Tesco's Basics and Sainsbury's Basics ranges, and cheap chicken.

In a social milieu which values reflexive individuality and diverse consumption, taste boundaries are ambivalent and fluid. Despite this, I have argued that they are still present, and through closer inspection it is possible to see how class is 'faintly written' (Savage 2003: 537) therein. Following Skeggs (2005), it is within this ambivalence that notions of disgust flourish: the proximity of the other becomes too close for comfort. When all foods are presented as culturally equal, social distance becomes distorted and harder to discern. Furthermore, when socially valued identities rely on personal investment of cultural forms, such as food, disgust and selectivity appear to be a necessary means of pushing the other away. Much of what participants did and said was premised on not being like 'them': a passive, uncritical consumer. The disgust levied at mass-produced or mainstream foods centred on these foods' lack of potential for individual investment. Disgust was largely directed at convenience foods suggesting that participants' relationship with 'good' food focused on enhancing its aesthetic value through material and symbolic labour. In the section that follows, I focus on this active relationship with food to consider how the sample domesticated food.

Domesticating food: processes of choice and restriction

'Actually cause I'm on my own today, I've actually got a ready meal from the supermarket (whispered).' (Harriet)

Later when showing me the fridge:

Harriet: Ok, well there's not much in here because like I said I succumbed slightly to the lure of the ready meal (laughs).

KG: Oh right, yes. Can I take a picture? (laughs).
Harriet: Yes, alright (laughs). I think I've got one of these.
KG: Ok, yeah.
Harriet: But normally this would *not* be in my fridge (laughs).
KG: No, I know.
Harriet: But basically ... jams, that's stock, that's homemade stock because I'm going to use that in something tomorrow probably. Otherwise it's fairly standard isn't it?

The concept of domestication provides a means of understanding the active ways that participants domesticate food from the consumer marketplace into the intimacy of the home. With the 'lure' of convenience foods ever-present, the enormous amounts of time and care that participants dedicated to preparing and sourcing the right kinds of food emerged as significant. Domestic food selection is a multi-linear process which extends out to the market, with the ideal end result being food which is homemade and individualized according to the habitus of the household. Distaste for mass-produced foods (particularly those bought from the homogenous, mass-consumption space of the supermarket) emerged as a powerful image in this research and an important reference from which my participants enacted distinction. 'Convenience' foods in particular were accorded little value since they remove the possibility of individual investment and personal touch. Under this framing, the ready meal, both mass-produced and a convenience, was positioned as the epitome of bad taste. As Harriet's quote highlights, the consumption of this food must be confessed to in hushed tones and positioned as something about which to feel guilty. Her mention that she 'succumbed to the lure' alludes to an admission of moral shortcoming. But despite the presence of the ready meal suggesting that somehow Harriet had slipped up, her critical justification and reflexive awareness about it not being the norm works to keep Harriet's good taste profile intact. Harriet's slippage can be offset because usually she makes an effort to invest in the food that she eats and feeds her household.

All participants displayed a heightened awareness about the importance of making an effort. From selecting the right foods in the marketplace through to expending time on food provisioning and particular ways of eating, infusing practices with aesthetic labour was important. Valued food is that which embodies a personal connection through its journey from market to plate, always understood in terms of choices: about quality, cost, and place of purchase, for instance. The overarching framing to these choices was the attainment of diversity. Taking the family meal as the final moment of domestication, I want to suggest that the value of this event lies in its function to display the habitus of the household through a personal connection with food. The staging of this occasion was articulated in relation to competing temporal forces but prioritized nonetheless as a means of doing family through food. Importantly though, the material and symbolic work undertaken to produce the food over which families bonded relied on a series of classed and gendered relationships. These function to reproduce the symbolic value of the family meal. Participants were explicit that family meals are important for family bonding.

Skeggs notes that formulations of reflexive individualism resonate with middle-class experience and perspectives (2004a). My research further complicates this picture: practice does not always mirror preference. While reflexive individualism emerged as powerful and worthy of perseverance, it certainly was not always participants' *experience*. The symbolism of the family meal is intimately tied to the unique and individual domesticity of a particular household. At the same time, it is distinguished in relation to its distance from homogenized foods produced externally to the household. Homemade food signifies a 'love of family' (Moisio et al 2004: 368). But it takes time to cook from scratch and to peruse the marketplace, and it takes time to plan and deliver the required diversity of 'good' food. It takes time and effort, in other words, to invest in the symbolic and material means to manage and restrict choice. The reproduction of these standards requires classed capital to both invest in and reproduce food, but it also requires the resource of time. It follows then that justifications around feeding households convenience foods were related to perceptions of compromising norms of care. Not cooking from scratch in these classed contexts denotes a lack of personal involvement in the production of food, and this was understood as contravening the standards of care through food. As such, the very investment in an ideal of 'good' food as that which reflects time and care devalues the shortcuts implied in convenience foods.

Predictably, this intimate care work through food is gendered. Just as Brannen, O'Connell and Mooney (2013) find, the responsibility for synchronizing the food-related time-space paths of the household lay with the female participants. They appeared disproportionately affected by the convenience and care antonym presented by Warde (1997). The guilt expressed by female participants when they made use of processed convenience foods showed the detrimental consequences experienced by women when the ideology of infusing food with time and care is compromised. Harriet is able to justify her ready meal because it is out of the ordinary that she is not feeding anyone else and therefore needs not expend any labour on cooking. Yet, as her explanation of her homemade stock suggests, in planning ahead for the following day's meal, she is still conducting the 'invisible' work of feeding (DeVault 1991).

A focus on life histories produced data highlighting that orientations to cooking and feeding as care were clearly laid down by my participants' mothers. This was reproduced by the participants in complex ways. Given the cohort's overall distance from childhood tastes, on the whole this generative learning manifested itself around food practices. The female participants were primarily responsible for managing feeding work which involved the delivery of health and diversity to the household; however, this was not passively performed. The women of this sample, and even the female partners of the male participants, were highly active in their roles of feeding the household. For instance, female participants said they cooked because they were better cooks, had more time or because of enjoyment. This involved making discerning food selections for themselves and the household in highly controlled and organized ways – for instance, planning variations in weekly meals through using cookbooks. Their roles as feeders are understood in terms of choice: they choose to feed, and they choose what to choose.

The navigation of choice involved in this feeding work is an important vehicle for the acquisition and display of culinary capital for the female participants, which draws on classed *and* gendered skills and knowledges. It culminates in a habitus which can display classed dispositions around strategic investment and gendered training around the successful delivery of domestic good food. Yet there was a lack of critical reflexivity in participants' narratives relating to the gendered responsibility of domestic feeding and feminized ways in which food management skills are generatively learnt. This is a powerful reminder of a symbolic violence which feminizes everyday feeding work as being central to knitting together familial relations. This has important implications for the reproduction of class and gender inequality because it tacitly naturalizes the classed reproduction of families through food as feminine. This process of naturalization is a fundamental way in which middle-class practice is reproduced as normal, even if it is sometimes out of reach for the most harried of the sample.

In participants' freezers, I was shown a number of homemade 'ready meals'. Being individually made from scratch, these meals did not offend classed and gendered standards of care. On the contrary, they were objects of value: indicative of a culmination of culinary and time management skills which prioritize efficiently delivering the household with good food within time constraints. The negative positioning of convenience food appears related to its mass production. The way many women in this sample discussed the conflict between handmade and convenience food suggests that they are all too aware of the importance of defending against an imagined, uncritical, mass-consuming other: the kind of woman who feeds the household ready meals. Of course, convenience foods were used in all households. But through their critical appraisal, participants were clear in communicating that these foods contravene the standards of good food. Drawing attention to their awareness of the need to distance themselves from mass-produced convenience foods has the effect of reproducing classed and gendered forms of individual investment through food as legitimate and valued. The social rewards attached to making active choices are constituted through their differentiation from being inactive, or lazy. Time and time again, the cohort positioned themselves as active through talk of 'making an effort' to find and cook the right ingredients, persevering to expand theirs and their children's tastes and preferences for diversity, and prioritizing eating together in fragmented time-space paths. Active personal involvement in the entire consumption process and subsequent domestic production of meaning clearly emerged as having value across the whole sample. As I will now go on to explore, this emphasis on active choices centralizes the self amid the competing forces of globalization, forces which were almost understood as a contaminating threat to domestic food practices.

Active consumers

> 'And I'm sure we could all eat better, you know we could eat less butter and do ... but we do basically give all our kids green vegetables and you know, there are still a lot of people who don't ... It's like, it's all over the newspapers all the time, how can you not, when you have children, realize that you need to make that an important thing? I don't know, it seems so ... nobody cannot know it anymore. It has to be a choice now.' (Carla)

As a single parent, the 'we' to which Carla refers is unclear, but I can only assume she means people like her. Relatedly, other people are knowingly making the wrong choices; they are knowingly *choosing* to ignore mediatized information. But like most participants, in navigating the social world, Carla also chooses to ignore much of the wealth of information on offer, specifically that which is aimed at the general public. Yet, ignoring certain information functions to display more, as opposed to less, knowledge for these participants. This is because they possess dominant capital, which legitimizes their performance. Participants distanced themselves from passively consuming mass-messaging, be it marketing messages (such as BOGOF), guidelines about best-before dates or government health messaging. But as I have suggested, their individualized understandings of themselves and their tastes and practices were similar across the sample, indicating that their tastes and practices are the result of a broader middle-class orientation to value individualism. These individualized identities conducted via food must be understood in relation to public narratives in which notions of the individual are made central matters of concern, such as public health policy. For example, publications by Public Health England (2016) aim to promote healthy (individual) *choices* around eating a balanced diet and exercising. Participants deployed public health narratives of self-control and balance when referring to their diets: using phrases such as 'everything in moderation', for instance.

Yet, on the whole, participants said they had no need to pay attention to public health messaging. This is important because unreflexively reproducing the individualistic nature of health messaging naturalizes a pre-disposition to be 'aware'. It highlights how dispositions to self-monitor are understood as an individual practical logic, as opposed to an embodied response to public health messaging. Positioning valued aspects of practices and perceptions as a function of individuality has the effect of positioning participants as self-conscious eaters. It masks the effects of class, which facilitates access to the resources which enable positioning as authentic and knowing. The contemporary foodscape is awash with concerns about the increase in junk food, the decline of cooking and fears that knowledge about cooking is no longer intergenerationally reproduced from parents to children. My research participants all drew on these public narratives despite their desire to draw on frames of individuality to make sense of themselves in their evaluation of food practices and choices. This reproduces classed practice as the result of individualized capacity: a function of who they are, rather than what they have access to. Individualizing tropes around good food leave little space for marginalized people to forge a positive identity for themselves, thus reproducing class privilege.

Conclusion

In this final chapter, I have assembled the findings of this research to offer an account of middle-class food practices and in so doing added layers of complexity to dominant accounts of 'good' food. I have sharpened the focus onto the perspectives and experiences of those with access to resources to attend to the ways in which classed advantages are reproduced. To do so, I have emphasized how the logic of practice inherent in middle-class decision-making relates to the strategic accumulation of capital. There was a homologous relationship between participants' social position and the classed resources they deployed to make sense of and justify their food choices. Cutting across every participant's understanding of good food was the sense that making an (individual) effort is mandatory. Yet, by probing the minutiae of daily domestic practices, we see how food taste preferences can be both compromised and facilitated by circumstances. In so doing, this research complicates the nature of individual *informed* choice, an ideology which is circulated in public and political imaginaries and relies on naïve assumptions about the relationship between knowing and doing.

This book is a response to calls that in order to address class inequality, it is necessary and important to address and critique the assumption that middle-class taste and practice carry inherent value (Savage 2003, 2015;

Skeggs 2004b, 2004a; Lawler 2005; Reay et al 2011). As Lawler (2005) emphasizes, just as whiteness and heterosexuality are saliently normalized, so too are middle-class dispositions. Using the examples of foodbanks, obesity and the circulation of food trends, this book began by explaining that class is relevant to *all* understandings of food in Great Britain. Yet there is a lack of scrutiny about how access to 'good' foods relies on the possession of multiple forms of capital. This implicitly marks 'good' food as classless.

Scrutinizing how class enables access to choice and valued forms of individuality is fundamental for effecting change in the field of food consumption. The consumer ideology of active and individual choice has highly moralizing consequences. It (re)produces a classed rhetoric which focuses on the individualized inadequacies of those cast as ignorant about 'correct' food choices. For example, Jamie Oliver is well documented for his crusade to educate the nation's poorest, whose children are 'eating chips and cheese out of Styrofoam containers, and behind them is a massive fucking TV' (Oliver in Deans 2013). The focus of this book has been to capture the classed processes which normalize ways of being and ways of eating and some of the relational ways which good food literally and metaphorically makes the middle-class embodied habitus. In so doing, I draw attention to the nuanced ways in which middle-class reproduction through food is implicitly marked as legitimate through its separation from the collective mass.

References

Abbots, E. (2016) 'Approaches to Food and Migration: Rootedness, Being and Belonging', in Klein, J. and Watson, J. (eds) *The Handbook of Food and Anthropology*, London: Bloomsbury, pp 115–132.

Allen, K. (2014). '"Blair's Children": Young Women as 'Aspirational Subjects' in the Psychic Landscape of Class', *The Sociological Review*, 62(4), 760–779.

Anguelovski, I. (2015) 'Healthy Food Stores, Greenlining and Food Gentrification: Contesting New Forms of Privilege, Displacement and Locally Unwanted Land Uses in Racially Mixed Neighborhoods', *International Journal of Urban and Regional Research*, 39(6), 1209–1230.

Armstrong, A. (2016) 'How Aldi Became the Magnet for the Middle Classes', The Telegraph, [online], 6 August. Available at: www.telegraph.co.uk/business/2016/08/06/how-aldi-became-the-magnet-for-the-middle-classes (Accessed: 27/6/2023).

Askegaard, S. and Brogärd, D. (2016) '"Authentic Food" and the Double Nature of Branding', in Cappellini, B., Marshall, D. and Parsons, E. (eds) *The Practice of the Meal: Food, Families and the Market Place*, Oxon: Routledge, pp 39–54.

Atkinson, W. and Deeming, C. (2015) 'Class and Cuisine in Contemporary Britain: The Social Space, the Space of Food and their Homology', *The Sociological Review*, 63(4), 876–896.

Backett-Milburn, K., Wills, W., Roberts, M.-L. and Lawton, J. (2010) 'Food, Eating and Taste: Parents' Perspectives on the Making of the Middle Class Teenager', *Social Science & Medicine*, 71(7), 1316–1323.

Ball, S.J. (2003) *Class Strategies and the Education Market: The Middle Classes and Social Advantage*, London: Routledge/Falmer.

Bauman, Z. (2009) 'Identity in the Globalizing World', in Elliott, A. and Du Gay, P. (eds) *Identity in Question*, London: Sage Publications, pp 1–13.

Beagan, B, Chapman, G.E., Johnston, J., McPhail, D., Power, E.M. and Vallianatos, H. (2015) *Acquired Tastes: Why Families Eat the Way They Do*. Vancouver: UBC Press.

Beagan, B., Chapman, G.E., D'Sylva, A. and Bassett, B.R. (2008) '"It's Just Easier for Me to Do It": Rationalizing the Family Division of Foodwork', *Sociology*, 42(4), 653–671.

Beardsworth, A. and Keil, T. (1992) 'Foodways in Flux: From Gastro-Anomy to Menu Pluralism?', *British Food Journal*, 94(7), 20–25.

Beck, U. (1992) *Risk Society: Towards a New Modernity*, London: Sage Publications.

Beck, U. and Beck-Gernsheim, E. (2009) 'Losing the Traditional: Individualization and "Precarious Freedoms"', in Elliott, A. and Du Gay, P. (eds) *Identity in Question*, London: Sage Publications, pp 13–36.

Bee, P. (2018) 'Eating: How Speed Affects Your Weight; Guzzling Your Food May Make You Obese. So Is the Reverse Also True? Peta Bee Asks the Experts', *The Times*, 6 March, London, pp 44–45.

Bennett, T. (2007) 'Habitus Clivé: Aesthetics and Politics in the Work of Pierre Bourdieu', *New Literary History*, 38(1), 201–228.

Bennett, T., Savage, M., Silva, E.B., Warde, A., Gayo-Cal, M. and Wright, D. (2009) *Culture, Class, Distinction*, London: Routledge.

Bennett, T. and Silva, E.B. (2004) 'Everyday Life in Contemporary Culture', in Bennett, T. and Silva, E.B. (eds) *Contemporary Culture and Everyday Life*, Durham: Routledge, pp 1–20.

Berker, T., Hartman, M., Punie, Y. and Ward, K. (2006) 'Introduction', in Berker, T., Hartman, M., Punie, Y. and Ward, K. (eds) *Domestication of Media and Technologies*, Berkshire: Open University Press, pp 1–17.

Blake, M., Mellor, J., Crane, L. and Osz, B. (2009) 'Eating in Time, Eating up Time', in Jackson, P. (ed) *Changing Families, Changing Food*, London: Palgrave Macmillan, pp 187–204.

Blunt, A. (2005) 'Cultural Geography: Cultural Geographies of Home', *Progress in Human Geography*, 29(4), 505–515.

Bourdieu, P. (1977) *Outline of a Theory of Practice*, Cambridge: Cambridge University Press.

Bourdieu, P. (1984) *Distinction: A Social Critique of the Judgement of Taste*, Oxon: Routledge.

Bourdieu, P. (1990a) *In Other Words: Essays Towards a Reflexive Sociology*, Cambridge: Polity Press.

Bourdieu, P. (1990b) *The Logic of Practice*, Cambridge: Polity Press.

Bourdieu, P. (1991) *Language and Symbolic Power*, Cambridge: Polity Press.

Bourdieu, P. (1996) 'On the Family as a Realized Category', *Theory, Culture & Society*, 13(3), 19–26.

Bourdieu, P. (2001) *Masculine Domination*, Stanford, CA: Stanford University Press.

Bourdieu, P. and Wacquant, L. (1992) *An Invitation to Reflexive Sociology*, Chicago, IL: University of Chicago Press.

Bourdieu, P. and Wacquant, L. (2013) 'Symbolic Capital and Social Classes', *Journal of Classical Sociology*, 13(2), 292–302.

Boyne, R. (2002) 'Bourdieu: From Class to Culture: In Memoriam Pierre Bourdieu 1930–2002', *Theory, Culture & Society*, 19(3), 117–128.

Bradley, H. (2018) 'Moving On Up? Social Mobility, Class and Higher Education' in Lawler, S. and Payne, G. (eds) *Social Mobility for the 21st Century: Everyone a Winner?*, Oxon: Routledge, pp 80–92.

Brannen, J., O'Connell, R. and Mooney, A. (2013) 'Families, Meals and Synchronicity: Eating Together in British Dual Earner Families', *Community, Work and Family*, 16(4), 417–434.

Broom, A., Hand, K. and Tovey, P. (2009) 'The Role of Gender, Environment and Individual Biography in Shaping Qualitative Interview Data', *International Journal of Social Research Methodology*, 12(1), 51–65.

Brownlie, D., Hewer, P. and Horne, S. (2005) 'Culinary Tourism: An Exploratory Reading of Contemporary Representations of Cooking', *Consumption Markets & Culture*, 8(1), 7–26.

Bugge, A.B. and Almås, R. (2006) 'Domestic Dinner: Representations and Practices of a Proper Meal Among Young Suburban Mothers', *Journal of Consumer Culture*, 6(2), 203–228.

Burn-Callander, R. (2015) 'How Charlie Bigham Convinced you to Spend an Extra £5 on Lasagne', *The Telegraph*, [online], 13 April. Available at: http://www.telegraph.co.uk/finance/businessclub/sales/11533032/How-Charlie-Bigham-convinced-you-to-spend-an-extra-2-on-a-lasagne.html (Accessed: 27/6/2023).

Cairns, K., Johnston, J. and Baumann, S. (2010) 'Caring About Food: Doing Gender in the Foodie Kitchen', *Gender & Society*, 24(5), 591–615.

Cairns, K., Johnston, J. and MacKendrick, N. (2013) 'Feeding the 'Organic Child': Mothering Through Ethical Consumption', *Journal of Consumer Culture*, 13(2), 97–118.

Cappellini B. and Parsons E. (2014) 'Constructing the Culinary Consumer: Transformative and Reflective Processes in Italian Cookbooks', *Consumption Markets & Culture*, 17(1), 71–99.

Cappellini, B. and Parsons, E. (2012) 'Sharing the Meal: Food Consumption and Family Identity', *Research in Consumer Behaviour*, 14, 109–128.

Cappellini, B and Parsons, E. (2013) 'Practising Thrift at Dinnertime: Mealtime Leftovers, Sacrifice and Family Membership', *The Sociological Review*, 60(2_ suppl), 121–134.

Cappellini, B., Parsons, E. and Harman, V. (2015) '"Right Taste, Wrong Place": Local Food Cultures, (Dis)identification and the Formation of Classed Identity', *Sociology*, 50(6), 1089–1105.

Cappellini, B., Marshall, D. and Parsons, E. (2016a) 'Concluding Remarks' in Cappellini, B., Marshall, D. and Parsons, E. (eds) *The Practice of the Meal: Food, Families and the Marketplace*, Oxon: Routledge, pp 245–247.

Cappellini, B., Marilli, A. and Parsons, E. (2016b) 'Working Your Way Down: Rebalancing Bourdieu's Capitals in Times of Need', in Cappellini, B., Marshall, D. and Parsons, E. (eds) *The Practice of the Meal: Food, Families and the Marketplace*, Oxon: Routledge, pp 43–56.

Cappellini, B. and Yen, D.A. (2013) 'Little Emperors in the UK: Acculturation and Food Over Time', *Journal of Business Research*, 66(8), 968–974.

Charles, N. and Kerr, M. (1988) *Women, Food and Families*, Manchester: Manchester University Press.

Coulangeon, P. (2015) 'Social Mobility and Musical Tastes: A Reappraisal of the Social Meaning of Taste Eclecticism', *Poetics*, 51, 54–68.

Crouch, G. (2021) 'How Posh Is Your Store Cupboard? The Best Jars and Tinned Food', The Times, 13 October [online]. Available at: https://www.thetimes.co.uk/article/how-posh-is-your-store-cupboard-the-best-jars-and-tinned-food-n55jgsnpg (Accessed: 27/6/2023).

Crouch, M. and O'Neill, G. (2000) 'Sustaining Identities? Prolegomena for Inquiry into Contemporary Foodways', *Social Science Information*, 39(1), 181–192.

Crozier, G., Reay, D., James, D., Jamieson, F., Beedell, P., Hollingworth, S. and Williams, K. (2008) 'White Middle-Class Parents, Identities, Educational Choice and the Urban Comprehensive School: Dilemmas, Ambivalence and Moral Ambiguity', *British Journal of Sociology of Education*, 29(3), 261–272.

Curley, R. (2018) 'TO AV AND TO HOLD: Middle-Class Millennials Now Proposing with AVOCADOS in Bizarre New Trend', *The Sun*, [online], 21 February. Available at: https://www.thesun.co.uk/news/5631426/middle-class-millennials-now-proposing-with-avocados-in-bizarre-new-trend/ (Accessed: 27/6/2023).

Curtis, P., James, A. and Ellis, K. (2009) '"She's Got a Really Good Attitude to Healthy Food ... Nannan's Drilled it into Her": Inter-generational Relations within Families', in Jackson, P. (ed) *Changing Families, Changing Food*, London: Palgrave Macmillan, pp 77–92.

Daenekindt, S. and Roose, H. (2014) 'Social Mobility and Cultural Dissonance', *Poetics*, 42, 82–97.

Daenekindt, S. and Roose, H. (2017) 'Ways of Preferring: Distinction Through the "What" and the "How" of Cultural Consumption', *Journal of Consumer Culture*, 17(1), 25–45.

Daloz, J-P. (2011) 'Towards the Cultural Contextualization of Social Distinction', *Journal of Cultural Economy*, 1(3), 305–320.

Daly, K. (2001) 'Deconstructing Family Time: From Ideology to Lived Experience', *Journal of Marriage and Family*, 63(2), 283–294.

Daniels, S., Glorieux, I., Minnen, J. and van Tienoven, T.P. (2012) 'More than Preparing a Meal? Concerning the Meanings of Home Cooking', *Appetite*, 58(3), 1050–1056.

Davis, T., Marshall, D., Hogg, M., Schneider, T. and Petersen, A. (2016) 'Consuming the family and the meal: representations of the family meal in women's magazines over 60 years' in Cappellini, B., Marshall, D. and Parsons, E. (eds) *The Practice of the Meal: Food, Families and the Market Place*, Oxon: Routledge, pp 137–150.

de Quetteville, H. (2022) 'How Aldi won over the supermarket snobs to become a middle class favourite', *Daily Telegraph*, September 13, [online]. Available at: https://www.telegraph.co.uk/business/2022/09/13/how-aldi-won-supermarket-snobs-become-middle-class-favourite (Accessed: 27/6/2023).

Deans, J. (2013) 'Jamie Oliver bemoans chips, cheese and giant TVs of modern-day poverty', *The Guardian*, August 27, [online]. Available at: http://www.theguardian.com/lifeandstyle/2013/aug/27/jamie-oliver-chips-cheese-modern-day-poverty (Accessed: 27/6/2023).

DeVault, M.L. (1991) *Feeding the Family: The Social Organization of Caring as Gendered Work*, Chicago: University of Chicago Press.

Douglas, M. (1975) 'Deciphering a Meal', *Daedalus*, 101(1), 61–81.

Ehlert, J. (2021) 'Food Consumption, Habitus and the Embodiment of Social Change: Making Class and Doing Gender in Urban Vietnam', *The Sociological Review*, 69(3), 681–701.

Ekstrom, K. (2016) 'The Multi-cultural Food Market: Grocery Stores Approaching Foreign-born Consumers in Sweden', in Cappellini, B., Marshall, D. and Parsons, E. (eds) *The Practice of the Meal: Food, Families and the Marketplace*, Oxon: Routledge, pp 57–74.

Emmison, M. (2003) 'Social Class and Cultural Mobility: Reconfiguring the Cultural Omnivore Thesis', *Journal of Sociology*, 39(3), 211–230.

Evans, D. (2012) 'Beyond the Throwaway Society: Ordinary Domestic Practice and a Sociological Approach to Household Food Waste', *Sociology*, 46(1), 41–56.

Evans, G. and Mellon, J. (2016) 'Identity, Awareness and Political Attitudes: Why Are We Still Working Class?' *British Social Attitudes*, 34rd report. London: NatCen Social Research.

Fischler, C. (1988) 'Food, Self and Identity', *Social Science Information*, 27, 275–293.

Fox, R. and Smith, G. (2011) 'Sinner Ladies and the Gospel of Good Taste: Geographies of Food, Class and Care', *Health & Place*, 17(2), 403–412.

Friedman, S. (2012) 'Cultural Omnivores or Culturally Homeless? Exploring the Shifting Cultural Identities of the Upwardly Mobile', *Poetics*, 40(5), 467–489.

Friedman, S. (2015) 'Habitus Clivé and the Emotional Imprint of Social Mobility', *Sociological Review*, 64(1), 129–147.

Friedman, S. and Savage, M. (2018) 'Time, Accumulation and Trajectory: Bourdieu and Social Mobility', in Lawler, S. and Payne, G. (eds) *Social Mobility for the 21ˢᵗ Century: Everyone a Winner?*, Oxon: Routledge, pp 67–79.

Friedman, S., O'Brien, D. and Laurison, D. (2017) '"Like Skydiving Without a Parachute": How Class Origin Shapes Occupational Trajectories in British Acting', *Sociology*, 51(5), 992–1010.

Friedman, S., O'Brien, D. and McDonald, I. (2021) 'Deflecting Privilege: Class Identity and the Intergenerational Self', *Sociology*, 55(4), 716–733.

Gallegos, D. (2005) 'Cookbooks as Manuals of Taste', in Bell, D. and Hollows, J. (eds) *Ordinary Lifestyles: Popular Media, Consumption and Taste*, Maidenhead: Open University Press, pp 99–110.

Garthwaite, K. (2016) *Hunger Pains: Life Inside Foodbank Britain*, Bristol: Policy Press.

Gibson, K., Pollard, T.M. and Moffatt, S. (2021) 'Social Prescribing and Classed Inequality: A Journey of Upward Health Mobility?' *Social Science & Medicine*, 280, 114037.

Giddens, A. (1991) *Modernity and Self-identity*, Cambridge: Polity Press.

Gidley, B. and Rooke, A. (2010) 'Asdatown: The Intersections of Classed Places and Identities', in Taylor, Y. (ed) *Classed Intersections: Spaces, Selves, Knowledges*, Farnham: Ashgate Publishing, pp 95–116.

Goffman, E. (1959) *The Presentation of Self in Everyday Life*, Garden City, NY: Doubleday & Co.

Gram, M. and Grønhøj, A. (2015) 'There is Usually Just One Friday a Week', *Food, Culture & Society*, 18(4), 547–567.

Green, T., Owen, J., Curtis, J., Smith, G., Ward, P. and Fisher, P. (2009) 'Making Healthy Families?' in Jackson, P (ed) *Changing Families, Changing Food*, London: Palgrave Macmillan UK, pp 205–225.

Haddon, L. (2018) 'Domestication and Social Constraints of ICT Use: Children's Engagement with Smartphones', in Vincent, J. and Haddon, L. (eds) *Smartphone Cultures*, Oxford: Routledge, pp 71–82.

Hall, S. (1996) 'Introduction: Who Needs "Identity"?' in Hall, S. and Du Gay, P. (eds) *Questions of Cultural Identity*, London: Sage Publications, pp 1–17.

Hammersley, M. and Atkinson, P. (2007) *Ethnography: Principles in Practice*, London: Routledge.

Hand, M. and Shove, E. (2004) 'Orchestrating Concepts: Kitchen Dynamics and Regime Change in Good Housekeeping and Ideal Home, 1922–2002', *Home Cultures*, 1(3), 235–256.

Hand, M., Shove, E. and Southerton, D. (2007) 'Home Extensions in the United Kingdom: Space, Time, and Practice', *Environment and Planning D: Society and Space*, 25(4), 668–681.

Hanquinet, L. (2017) 'Exploring Dissonance and Omnivorousness: Another Look into the Rise of Eclecticism', *Cultural Sociology*, 11(2), 165–187.

Harman, V. and Cappellini, B. (2015) 'Mothers on Display: Lunchboxes, Social Class and Moral Accountability', *Sociology*, 49(4), 764–781.

Haukanes, H. (2007) 'Sharing Food, Sharing Taste? Consumption Practices, Gender Relations and Individuality in Czech Families', *Anthropology of Food*, (S3), 1–11.

Hewer, P. (2016) 'Fraught Contexts and Mediated Culinary Practices: Ontological Practices and Politics', in Cappellini, B., Marshall, D. and Parsons, E. (eds) *The Practice of the Meal: Food, Families and the Market Place*, Oxon: Routledge, pp 123–134.

Hochschild, A.R. (1997) *The Time Bind: When Work Becomes Home and Home Becomes Work*, New York: Metropolitan Books.

Hollands, R. and Chatterton, P. (2002) 'Changing Times for an Old Industrial City: Hard Times, Hedonism and Corporate Power in Newcastle's Nightlife', *City*, 6(3), 291–315.

Holtzman, J. D. (2006) 'Food and Memory', *Annual Review of Anthropology*, 35(1), 361–378.

Hsu, E.L. (2015) 'The Slow Food Movement and Time Shortage: Beyond the Dichotomy of Fast or Slow', *Journal of Sociology*, 51(3), 628–642.

Hurdley, R. (2006) 'Dismantling Mantelpieces: Narrating Identities and Materializing Culture in the Home', *Sociology*, 40(4), 717–733.

Jackson, P. (ed) (2009) *Changing Families, Changing Food*, London: Palgrave Macmillan UK.

Jackson, P. (2010) 'Food Stories: Consumption in an Age of Anxiety', *Cultural Geographies*, 17(2), 147–165.

Jackson, E. and Benson, M. (2014) 'Neither "Deepest, Darkest Peckham" nor "Run-of-the-Mill" East Dulwich: The Middle Classes and their "Others" in an Inner-London Neighbourhood', *International Journal of Urban and Regional Research*, 38(4), 1195–1210.

Jackson, P. and Meah, A. (2019) 'Taking Humor Seriously in Contemporary Food Research', *Food, Culture & Society*, 22(3), 262–279.

Jackson, P. and Viehoff, V. (2016) 'Reframing Convenience Food', *Appetite*, 98(SupplC), 1–11.

Jackson, P., Olive, S. and Smith, G. (2009) 'Myths of the Family Meal: Re-Reading Edwardian Life Histories', in Jackson, P. (ed) *Changing Families, Changing Food*, Basingstoke: Palgrave-Macmillan, pp 131–145.

James, A. (1997) 'How British is British Food?' in Caplan, P. (ed) *Food, Health and Identity*, London: Routledge, pp 71–86.

James, A. and Curtis, P. (2010) 'Family Displays and Personal Lives', *Sociology*, 44(6), 1163–1180.

Jenkins, R. (1982) 'Pierre Bourdieu and the Reproduction of Determinism', *Sociology*, 16(2), 270–281.

Jensen, T. (2018) *Parenting the Crisis: The Cultural Politics of Parent-blame*. Bristol: Policy Press.

Johnston, J., Rodney, A. and Szabo, M. (2012) 'Place, Ethics, and Everyday Eating: A Tale of Two Neighbourhoods', *Sociology*, 46(6), 1091–1108.

Johnston, J. and Szabo, M. (2011) 'Reflexivity and the Whole Foods Market Consumer: The Lived Experience of Shopping for Change', *Agriculture and Human Values*, 28(3), 303–319.

Johnston, J., Szabo, M. and Rodney, A. (2011) 'Good Food, Good People: Understanding the Cultural Repertoire of Ethical Eating', *Journal of Consumer Culture*, 11(3), 293–318.

Johnston, J. and Baumann, S. (2007) 'Democracy Versus Distinction: A Study of Omnivorousness in Gourmet Food Writing', *American Journal of Sociology*, 113(1), 165–204.

Johnston, J. and Baumann, S. (2014) *Foodies: Democracy and Distinction in the Gourmet Foodscape*, London: Routledge.

Kennedy, E.H., Baumann, S., and Johnston, J. (2019) 'Eating for Taste and Eating for Change: Ethical Consumption as a High-Status Practice', *Social Forces*, 98(1), 381–402.

Kierans, C. and Haeney, J. (2010) 'The "Social Life" of Scouse: Understanding Contemporary Liverpool Through Changing Food Practices', *Cultural Sociology*, 4(1), 101–122.

Klasson, M. and Ulver, S. (2015) 'Masculinising Domesticity: An Investigation of Men's Domestic Foodwork', *Journal of Marketing Management*, 31(15–16), 1652–1675.

Kusenbach, M. (2003) 'Street Phenomenology: The Go-Along as Ethnographic Research Tool', *Ethnography*, 4(3), 455–485.

Lawler, S. (1999) '"Getting Out and Getting Away": Women's Narratives of Class Mobility', *Feminist Review,* 63(1), 3–24.

Lawler, S. (2002) 'Mobs and Monsters: Independent Man Meets Paulsgrove Woman', *Feminist Theory*, 3(1), 103–113.

Lawler, S. (2004) 'Rules of Engagement: Habitus, Power and Resistance', *The Sociological Review,* 52(s2), 110–128.

Lawler, S. (2005) 'Disgusted Subjects: The Making of Middle-Class Identities', *The Sociological Review*, 53(3), 429–446.

Lawler, S. (2011) 'The Middle Classes and their Aristocratic Others: Culture as Nature in Classification Struggles', in Warde, A. (ed) *Cultural Consumption, Classification and Power*, Oxon: Routledge, pp 4–20.

Lawler, S. (2014) *Identity: Sociological Perspectives*, Cambridge: Polity Press.

Lawler, S. (2018) 'Social Mobility Talk: Class-Making in Neo-Liberal Times', in Lawler, S. and Payne, G. (eds) *Social Mobility for the 21st Century: Everyone a Winner?*, Oxon: Routledge, pp 118–132.

Lehmann, W. (2014) 'Habitus Transformation and Hidden Injuries: Successful Working-class University Students', *Sociology of Education*, 87(1), 1–15.

Loveday, V. (2015) 'Working-class Participation, Middle-class Aspiration? Value, Upward Mobility and Symbolic Indebtedness in Higher Education', *The Sociological Review*, 63(3), 570–588.

Lupton, D. (1996) *Food, the Body and the Self*, London: Sage Publications.

Mallett, S. (2004) 'Understanding Home: A Critical Review of the Literature', *The Sociological Review*, 52(1), 62–89.

Mallman, M. (2017) 'Not Entirely at Home: Upward Social Mobility and Early Family Life', *Journal of Sociology*, 53(1), 18–31.

Mallman, M. (2018) 'Disruption in the Working-Class Family: The Early Origins of Social Mobility and *Habitus Clivé*', in Lawler, S. and Payne, G. (eds) *Social Mobility for the 21st Century: Everyone a Winner?*, Oxon: Routledge, pp 25–36.

Mancino, L. and Newman, C. (2006) *'Who's Cooking? Time Spent Preparing Food by Gender, Income and Household Composition'*, *2006 Annual meeting, July 23–26*, Long Beach, CA, American Agricultural Economics Association.

Mannay, D. and Morgan, M. (2015) 'Doing Ethnography or Applying a Qualitative Technique? Reflections from the "Waiting Field"', *Qualitative Research*, 15(2), 166–182.

Marshall, D., Cappellini, B. and Parsons, E. (2016) 'Introduction: The Practice of the Meal', in Cappellini, B., Marshall, D. and Parsons, E. (eds) *The Practice of the Meal: Food, Families and the Market Place*, Oxon: Routledge, pp 179–194.

McKenzie, J.S. and Watts, D. (2020) '"Things Like Tinned Burgers and Tinned Macaroni, I Ate as a Kid – I Would Not Look at It Twice!" Understanding Changing Eating Practices across the Lifecourse', *Food, Culture & Society*, 23(1), 66–85.

McNay, L. (2008) *Against Recognition*, Cambridge: Polity Press.

Meah, A. (2016) 'Extending the Contested Spaces of the Modern Kitchen', *Geography Compass*, 10(2), 41–55.

Meah, A. and Jackson, P. (2016) 'Re-imagining the Kitchen as a Site of Memory', *Social & Cultural Geography*, 17(4), 511–532.

Meah, A. and Jackson, P. (2017) 'Convenience as Care: Culinary Antinomies in Practice', *Environment and Planning A: Economy and Space*, 49(9), 2065–2081.

Mellor, J., Blake, M. and Crane, L. (2010) '"When I'm Doing a Dinner Party I Don't Go for the Tesco Cheeses": Gendered Class Distinctions, Friendship and Home Entertaining', *Food, Culture & Society*, 13(1), 115–134.

Mellor, J., Ingram, N., Abrahams, J. and Beedell, P. (2014) 'Class Matters in the Interview Setting? Positionality, Situatedness and Class', *British Educational Research Journal*, 40(1), 135–149.

Mennell, S. (1985) *All Manners of Food: Eating and Taste in England and France from the Middle Ages to the Present*, Oxford: Basil Blackwell.

Moisio, R., Arnould, E. and Price, L. (2004) 'Between Mothers and Markets: Constructing Family Identity through Homemade Food', *Journal of Consumer Culture*, 4(3), 361–384.

Moore, M. (2019) 'Let Fat People Die to Save NHS Money, Says Michael Buerk', *The Times*, 6 August [online], Available at: https://www.thetimes.co.uk/article/9c05cc52-b7c4-11e9-9ed1-57176c9fe03e (Accessed: 27/6/2023).

Murcott, A. (1997) 'Family Meals – a Thing of the Past?' in Caplan, P. (ed) *Food, Health and Identity*, London: Routledge, pp 32–49.

Murcott, A. (2012) 'Lamenting the "Decline of the Family Meal" as a Moral Panic? Methodological Reflections', *Recherches Sociologiques et Anthropologiques*, (43–1), 97–118.

Naccarato, P. and LeBesco, K. (2012) *Culinary Capital*. London: Berg.

Nettleton, S. and Uprichard, E. (2011) '"A Slice of Life": Food Narratives and Menus from Mass-Observers in 1982 and 1945', *Sociological Research Online*, [online], 16(2). Available at: http://www.socresonline.org.uk/16/12/15.html (Accessed: 27/6/2023).

Neuman, N., Gottzén, L. and Fjellström, C. (2017) 'Masculinity and the Sociality of Cooking in Men's Everyday Lives', *The Sociological Review*, 65(4), 816–831.

NHS Digital (2020) National Child Measurement Programme, England 2019/20 School Year, Health and Social Care Information Centre [online]. Available at: https://digital.nhs.uk/data-and-information/publications/statistical/national-child-measurement-programme/2019-20-school-year (Accessed: 27/6/2023).

Ochs, E and Kremer-Sadlik, T. (2015) 'How Postindustrial Families Talk', *Annual Review of Anthropology*, 44(1), 87–103.

O'Connell, R., Knight, A. and Brannen, J. (2019) 'Below the Breadline: Families and Food in Austerity Britain', in Česnuitytė, V. and Meil, G. (eds) *Families in Economically Hard Times*, Emerald Publishing Limited, Bingley, pp 167–185.

O'Connell, R. and Brannen, J. (2016) *Food, Families and Work*. London: Bloomsbury Academic.

Office for National Statistics (2022) 'Ethnic group, England and Wales: Census 2021' [online], Available at: https://www.ons.gov.uk/peoplepopulationandcommunity/culturalidentity/ethnicity/bulletins/ethnicgroupenglandandwales/census2021 (Accessed: 28/6/2023).

Oleschuk, M. (2017) 'Foodies of Color: Authenticity and Exoticism in Omnivorous Food Culture', *Cultural Sociology*, 11(2), 217–233.

Ollivier, M. (2008) 'Modes of Openness to Cultural Diversity: Humanist, Populist, Practical, and Indifferent', *Poetics*, 36(2–3), 120–147.

Oncini, F. (2020) 'Cuisine, Health and Table Manners: Food Boundaries and Forms of Distinction among Primary School Children', *Sociology*, 54(3), 626–642.

Owen, J., Metcalfe, A., Dryden, C. and Shipton, G. (2010) '"If They Don't Eat It, It's Not a Proper Meal": Images of Risk and Choice in Fathers' Accounts of Family Food Practices', *Health, Risk & Society*, 12(4), 395–406.

Oxford English Dictionary (2023) 'Omnivore, n.', [online], Oxford University Press. Available at: http://www.oed.com/view/Entry/236697 (Accessed: 27/6/2023).

Paddock, J. (2016) 'Positioning Food Cultures: "Alternative" Food as Distinctive Consumer Practice', *Sociology*, 50(6), 1039–1055.

Parsons, J. (2014) '"Cheese and Chips Out of Styrofoam Containers": An Exploration of Taste and Cultural Symbols of Appropriate Family Foodways', *M/C Journal*, 17(1).

Parsons, J. (2015) *Gender, Class and Food: Families, Bodies and Health*, London: Palgrave MacMillan.

Parsons, J. (2016) 'When Convenience is Inconvenient: "Healthy" Family Foodways and the Persistent Intersectionalities of Gender and Class', *Journal of Gender Studies*, 25(4), 382–397.

Peterson, R.A. (1992) 'Understanding Audience Segmentation: From Elite and Mass to Omnivore and Univore', *Poetics*, 21(4), 243–258.

Peterson, R.A. and Kern, R.M. (1996) 'Changing Highbrow Taste: From Snob to Omnivore', *American Sociological Review*, 61(5), 900–907.

Pink, S. (2004) *Home Truths: Gender, Domestic Objects and Everyday Life*, Oxford: Berg.

Pink, S., Mackley, K.L. and Moroşanu, R. (2015) 'Hanging Out at Home: Laundry as a Thread and Texture of Everyday Life', *International Journal of Cultural Studies*, 18(2), 209–224.

Plesner, U. (2011) 'Studying Sideways: Displacing the Problem of Power in Research Interviews with Sociologists and Journalists', *Qualitative Inquiry*, 17(6), 471–482.

Potter, L. and Westall, C. (2013) 'Neoliberal Britain's Austerity Foodscape: Home Economics, Veg Patch Capitalism and Culinary Temporality', *New Formations*, 80–81, 155–178.

Probyn, E. (2000) *Carnal Appetites: FoodSexIdentities*, London: Routledge.

Public Health England (2016) 'The Eatwell Guide: Helping You Eat a Healthy, Balanced Diet', [online], v2, Crown Copyright. Available at: https://www.gov.uk/government/uploads/system/uploads/attachment_data/file/551502/Eatwell_Guide_booklet.pdf (Accessed: 27/6/2023).

Reay, D. (1998) *Class Work: Mother's Involvement in their Children's Primary Schooling*, London: UCL Press.

Reay, D. (2004) '"It's All Becoming a Habitus": Beyond the Habitual Use of Habitus in Educational Research', *British Journal of Sociology of Education*, 25(4), 431–444.

Reay, D. (2005) 'Beyond Consciousness? The Psychic Landscape of Social Class', *Sociology*, 39(5), 911–928.

Reay, D. (2013) 'Social Mobility, a Panacea for Austere Times: Tales of Emperors, Frogs, and Tadpoles', *British Journal of Sociology of Education*, 34(5–6), 660–677.

Reay, D. (2017) *Miseducation: Inequality, Education and the Working Classes*, Bristol: Polity Press.

Reay, D. (2018) 'The Cruelty of Social Mobility: Individual Success at the Cost of Collective Failure', in Lawler, S. and Payne, G. (eds) *Social Mobility for the 21st Century: Everyone a Winner?*, Oxon: Routledge, 146–157.

Reay, D., Crozier, G. and James, D. (2011) *White Middle Class Identities and Urban Schooling. Identity Studies in the Social Sciences*, New York: Palgrave Macmillan.

Reay, D., Crozier, G. and Clayton, J. (2009) '"Strangers in Paradise"? Working-class Students in Elite Universities', *Sociology*, 43(6), 1103–1121.

Salter, K. (2016) 'Oat Cuisine: How Porridge got Posh', *The Guardian*, [online], 26 February. Available at: https://www.theguardian.com/life andstyle/wordofmouth/2016/feb/26/oat-cuisine-how-porridge-got-posh (27/6/2023).

Savage, M. (2000) *Class Analysis and Social Transformation*, Buckingham: Open University Press.

Savage, M. (2003) 'Review Essay: A New Class Paradigm?' *British Journal of Sociology of Education*, 24(4), 535–541.

Savage, M. (2015) 'Introduction to Elites: From the 'Problematic of the Proletariat' to a Class Analysis of "Wealth Elites"', *The Sociological Review*, 63(2), 223–239.

Savage, M., Cunningham, N., Devine, F., Friedman, S., Laurison, D., McKenzie, L. et al. (2015) *Social Class in the 21st Century*, UK: Penguin Books.

Schatzki, T. (2009) 'Timespace and the Organization of Social Life', in Shove, E., Trentmann, F. and Wilk, R. (eds) *Time, Consumption and Everyday Life: Practice, Materiality and Culture*, Oxford: Berg, pp 35–48.

Serre, D. and Wagner, A.-C. (2015) 'For a Relational Approach to Cultural Capital: A Concept Tested by Changes in the French Social Space', *The Sociological Review*, 63(2), 433–450.

Shildrick, T. (2018) *Poverty Propaganda: Exploring the Myths*. Bristol: Policy Press.

Shove, E. and Southerton D. (2000) 'Defrosting the Freezer: From Novelty to Convenience: A Narrative of Normalization', *Journal of Material Culture*, 5(3), 301–319.

Silva, E.B. (2005) 'Gender, Home and Family in Cultural Capital Theory', *The British Journal of Sociology*, 56(1), 83–103.

Silverstone, R. (2005) 'Domesticating Domestication: Reflections on the Life of a Concept', in Berker, T., Hartmann, M., Punie, Y. and Ward, K. (eds) *Domestication of Media and Technologies*, Maidenhead: Open University Press, pp 229–248.

Silverstone, R. and Haddon, L. (1996) 'Design and the Domestication of Information and Communication Technologies: Technical Change and Everyday Life', in Mansell, R. and Silverstone, R. (eds) *Communication by Design: The Politics of Information and Communication Technologies*, Oxford: Oxford University Press, pp 44–74.

Skeer, M.R. and Ballard, E.L. (2013) 'Are Family Meals as Good for Youth as We Think They Are? A Review of the Literature on Family Meals as They Pertain to Adolescent Risk Prevention', *Journal of Youth and Adolescence*, 42(7), 943–963.

Skeggs, B. (1997) *Formations of Class and Gender: Becoming Respectable*, London: Sage Publications.

Skeggs, B. (2002) 'Techniques for Telling the Reflexive Self', in May, T. (ed) *Qualitative Research in Action*, London: Sage Publications, pp 349–375.

Skeggs, B. (2004a) *Class, Self, Culture*, London, Routledge.

Skeggs, B. (2004b) 'Exchange, Value and Affect: Bourdieu and "the Self"', *The Sociological Review*, 52(s2), 75–95.

Skeggs, B. (2005) 'The Making of Class and Gender Through Visualizing Moral Subject Formation', *Sociology*, 39(5), 965–982.

Skeggs, B. (2011) 'Imagining Personhood Differently: Person Value and Autonomist Working-Class Value Practices', *Sociological Review*, 59(3), 496–513.

Skeggs, B. and Wood, H. (2008) 'The Labour of Transformation and Circuits of Value 'around' Reality Television', *Continuum*, 22(4), 559–572.

Smith, D. (1989) *Complete Illustrated Cookery Course*, London: BBC Books Ltd.

Smith Maguire, J. (2018) 'The Taste for the Particular: A Logic of Discernment in an Age of Omnivorousness', *Journal of Consumer Culture*, 18(1), 3–20.

Southerton, D. (2003) '"Squeezing Time": Allocating Practices, Coordinating Networks and Scheduling Society', *Time & Society*, 12(1), 5–25.

Southerton, D. (2006) 'Analysing the Temporal Organization of Daily Life: Social Constraints, Practices and their Allocation', *Sociology*, 40(3), 435–454.

Spencer, C. (2002) *British Food: An Extraordinary Thousand Years of History*, New York: Columbia University Press.

Spencer, L. and Pahl, R. (2006) *Rethinking Friendship: Hidden Solidarities Today*, Princeton, NJ: Princeton University Press.

Spracklen, K. (2011) 'Dreaming of Drams: Authenticity in Scottish Whisky Tourism as an Expression of Unresolved Habermasian Rationalities', *Leisure Studies*, 30(1), 99–116.

Spracklen, K., Laurencic, J. and Kenyon, A. (2013) '"Mine's a Pint of Bitter": Performativity, Gender, Class and Representations of Authenticity in Real-ale Tourism', *Tourist Studies*, 13(3), 304–321.

Stenning, A., Smith, A., Rochovská, A. and Świątek, D. (2010) *Domesticating Neo-liberalism: Spaces of Economic Practice and Social Reproduction in Post-Socialist Cities*, Chichester: Wiley-Blackwell.

Sullivan, O. (1997) 'Time Waits for No (Wo)man: An Investigation of the Gendered Experience of Domestic Time', *Sociology*, 31(2), 221–239.

Szabo, M. (2012) 'Foodwork or Foodplay? Men's Domestic Cooking, Privilege and Leisure', *Sociology*, 47(4), 623–638.

Szabo, M. (2014) 'Men Nurturing Through Food: Challenging Gender Dichotomies Around Domestic Cooking', *Journal of Gender Studies*, 23(1), 18–31.

Theophano, J. (2002) *Eat My Words: Reading Women's Lives Through the Cookbooks They Wrote*, New York: Palgrave.

Thompson, A. (2017) 'High-Protein Food Sales Are Soaring as Britons Become Increasingly Health-Conscious', MailOnline, [online], 23 October. Available at: http://www.dailymail.co.uk/health/article-5007 535/High-protein-food-sales-soaring.html (Accessed: 27/6/2023).

Thompson, C.J. (1996) 'Caring Consumers: Gendered Consumption Meanings and the Juggling Lifestyle', *Journal of Consumer Research*, 22(4), 388–407.

Trussell Trust (2022) End of Year Stats [online], Available at: https://www.trusselltrust.org/news-and-blog/latest-stats/end-year-stats/ (Accessed: 27/6/2023).

Turner, A. (1995) 'Prepacked Food Labelling: Past, Present and Future', *British Food Journal*, 97(5), 23–31.

Tyler, I. (2008) 'Chav Mum Chav Scum', *Feminist Media Studies*, 8(1), 17–34.

Tyler, I. (2015) 'Classificatory Struggles: Class, Culture and Inequality in Neoliberal Times', *The Sociological Review*, 63(2), 493–511.

Wacquant, L. (2013) 'Symbolic Power and Group-making: On Pierre Bourdieu's Reframing of Class', *Journal of Classical Sociology*, 13(2), 274–291.

Waitrose and Partners (2021) Food and Drink Report, 2021–22, [online]. Available at: https://www.docdroid.net/qK7pJYi/waitrose-food-drink-report-21-22-pdf (Accessed: 27/6/2023).

Waitt, G. and Phillips, C. (2016) 'Food Waste and Domestic Refrigeration: A Visceral and Material Approach', *Social & Cultural Geography*, 17(3), 359–379.

Warde, A. (1994) 'Consumption, Identity-Formation and Uncertainty', *Sociology*, 28(4), 877–898.

Warde, A. (1997) *Consumption, Food and Taste*, London: Sage Publications.

Warde, A. (1999) 'Convenience Food: Space and Timing', *British Food Journal*, 101(7), 518–527.

Warde, A. (2004) 'Practice and Field: Revising Bourdieusian Concepts', Centre for Research on Innovation & Competition Discussion Paper, No. 65, April, Manchester: University of Manchester.

Warde, A. (2008) 'Dimensions of a Social Theory of Taste', *Journal of Cultural Economy*, 1(3), 321–336.

Warde, A. (2014) 'After Taste: Culture, Consumption and Theories of Practice', *Journal of Consumer Culture*, 14(3), 279–303.

Warde, A. (2017) *Consumption: A Sociological Analysis*, London: Palgrave Macmillan.

Warde, A., Cheng, S.-L., Olsen, W. and Southerton, D. (2007) 'Changes in the Practice of Eating: A Comparative Analysis of Time-Use', *Acta Sociologica*, 50(4), 363–385.

Warde, A., Wright, D. and Gayo-Cal, M. (2008) 'The Omnivorous Orientation in the UK', *Poetics*, 36(2–3), 148–165.

Warde, A. and Gayo-Cal, M. (2009) 'The Anatomy of Cultural Omnivorousness: The Case of the United Kingdom', *Poetics*, 37(2), 119–145.

Warde, A. and Martens, L. (2000) *Eating Out: Social Differentiation, Consumption, and Pleasure*, Cambridge: Cambridge University Press.

Warde, A., Martens, L. and Olsen, W. (1999) 'Consumption and the Problem of Variety: Cultural Omnivorousness, Social Distinction and Dining Out', *Sociology*, 33(01), 105–127.

Warde, A., Whillans, J. and Paddock, J. (2017) 'On the Slow Pace of Culture Change and Prospects for the Improvement of Men', *Discover Society*, [online], 6 December. Available at: https://discoversociety.org/2017/12/06/on-the-slow-pace-of-culture-change-and-prospects-for-the-improvement-of-men/ (Accessed: 27/6/2023).

Warde, A., Wright, D. and Gayo-Cal, M. (2008) 'The Omnivorous Orientation in the UK', *Poetics*, 36(2), 148–165.

Warde, A. and Yates, L. (2017) 'Understanding Eating Events: Snacks and Meal Patterns in Great Britain', *Food, Culture & Society*, 20(1), 15–36.

Weiss, B. (2012) 'Configuring the Authentic Value of Real Food: Farm-to-Fork, Snout-to-Tail, and Local Food Movements', *American Ethnologist*, 39(3), 614–626.

Wilk, R. (2006) 'From Wild Seeds to Artisanal Cheese', in Wilk, R. (ed) *Fast Food/Slow Food: The Cultural Economy of the Global Food System*, Lanham, MD: Altamira Press, pp 13–27.

Wilk, R. (2010) 'Power at the Table: Food Fights and Happy Meals', *Cultural Studies ↔ Critical Methodologies*, 10(6), 428–436.

Wills, W. and O'Connell, R. (2018) 'Children's and Young People's Food Practices in Contexts of Poverty and Inequality', *Children and Society*, 32(3), 169–173.

Wills, W., Dickinson, A., Meah, A. and Short, F. (2016) 'Reflections on the Use of Visual Methods in a Qualitative Study of Domestic Kitchen Practices', *Sociology*, 50(3), 470–485.

Yalvaç, N.S. and Hazır, I. (2021) 'Do Omnivores Perform Class Distinction? A Qualitative Inspection of Culinary Tastes, Boundaries and Cultural Tolerance', *Sociology*, 55(3), 469–486.

Yates, L. and Warde, A. (2017) 'Eating Together and Eating Alone: Meal Arrangements in British Households', *The British Journal of Sociology*, 68(1), 97–118.

Zukin, S. (2008) 'Consuming Authenticity', *Cultural Studies*, 22(5), 724–748.

Index

References to tables appear in **bold** type.